I wish this book had been available for me to read some thirty years ago! Both Jonathan and Rob pull no punches in describing the challenges and difficulties that arise from leaving active homosexual practice in obedience to God's life guidelines following salvation. Using their own stories, and those of others, the authors offer many spiritual and practical ways in which a man or woman with same-sex attraction can embrace their weaknesses as well as their strengths and offer both to the glory of God. I wholeheartedly recommend *Satisfaction Guaranteed*.

Jeanette Howard, speaker and author of Out of Egypt, Into the Promised Land *and* Dwelling in the Land: Bringing same-sex attraction under the lordship of Christ

Jonathan and Rob don't dodge any bullets! They don't skirt round the issues or minimize the challenges of same-sex attraction but graciously, honestly and biblically remind us all that lasting satisfaction is found only in Christ. Dealing with issues such as identity, freedom and intimacy, *Satisfaction Guaranteed* is a must-read for same-sex attracted Christians, their friends and church leaders. Highly recommended.

Elizabeth McQuoid, Commissioning Editor at Keswick Ministries and speaker at women's events

We need all the wisdom and insight we can get in these revisionist days, and Jonathan Berry has provided a helpful and heartfelt resource. Holding gladly to the path of God's word, yet more aware than most of the tempting detours, he walks us down the path of true faithfulness and ultimate satisfaction found in Jesus Christ.

Simon Manchester, Senior Minister, St Thomas' Anglican Church, North Sydney

A wonderful blend of personal story, biblical wisdom and practical help for Christians experiencing same-sex attraction and for those who want to journey supportively alongside them.

John Risbridger, Minister and Team Leader, Above Bar Church, Southampton, and Chair of Keswick Ministries

Jonathan and Rob's stories are those we're missing in this whole area – Christians who have experienced the 'gay lifestyle' but have found greater satisfaction in the Lord Jesus. They need to be heard. And their honesty is going to be incredibly helpful for people grappling with the same issues. It was for me.

Ed Shaw, Co-Founder of Living Out and author of The Plausibility Problem

Jonathan and Rob's book *Satisfaction Guaranteed* offers a compelling account of how the gospel of Christ relates to people struggling with same-sex attraction. The authors are able to bring a powerful blend of vulnerable experiences and robust theological reflection into conversation with one another. If you want a fluffy memoir or a cold scholarly analysis of homosexuality, then go elsewhere. But if you want a raw reflection of how the gospel compels two same-sex attracted Christians to find their identity in Jesus, then this book is for you.

Preston Sprinkle, Vice President, Eternity Bible College's Boise extension and author of People to Be Loved: Why homosexuality is not just an issue

ivp

SATISFACTION GUARANTEED

A FUTURE AND A HOPE FOR SAME-SEX ATTRACTED CHRISTIANS

JONATHAN BERRY

WITH ROB WOOD

INTER-VARSITY PRESS
36 Causton Street, London SW1P 4ST, England
Email: ivp@ivpbooks.com
Website: www.ivpbooks.com

British Library Cataloguing-in-Publication Data
A catalogue record for this book is available from the British Library.

ISBN: 978–1–78359–424–5
eBook ISBN: 978–1–78359–476–4

Set in Dante 12/15pt
Typeset in Great Britain by CRB Associates, Potterhanworth, Lincolnshire
Printed in Great Britain by Ashford Colour Press Ltd, Gosport, Hampshire

*Inter-Varsity Press publishes Christian books that are true to the Bible and that
communicate the gospel, develop discipleship and strengthen the church for its mission
in the world.*

*IVP originated within the Inter-Varsity Fellowship, now the Universities and Colleges
Christian Fellowship, a student movement connecting Christian Unions in universities
and colleges throughout Great Britain, and a member movement of the International
Fellowship of Evangelical Students. Website: www.uccf.org.uk. That historic association
is maintained, and all senior IVP staff and committee members subscribe to the UCCF
Basis of Faith.*

*This book is dedicated to John and Mary, who
led me to faith in Christ and modelled the Christian life to me.
Also to each of our families, who lovingly brought us up and
have stood by us in all the changing scenes of life.*

CONTENTS

DISCLAIMER

While telling our own true personal stories, both Rob and I have carefully changed the names and identifying details of the other people we've mentioned. We have shared pastoral conversations with the kind permission of those concerned, but again, names and details have been altered. On a couple of occasions we have created a composite character, based on an amalgamation of real conversations with several individuals. All of this is in the interests of guarding the privacy of others and respecting pastoral and professional confidentiality.

ACKNOWLEDGMENTS

Warm thanks to all the trustees, and my colleagues, at True Freedom Trust who encouraged and enthusiastically supported me in this writing project. The whole staff team pulled together and took on extra responsibility, freeing me up to write. I'm also thankful to various friends and colleagues who have read through partial manuscripts and offered constructive feedback. And I'm grateful to the fantastic team at IVP who commissioned the book and were willing to nurture a new author with great patience. In particular, our editor Eleanor Trotter has provided so many helpful insights and lots of constructive feedback. And she tenaciously, yet gently, encouraged me to keep improving the manuscript.

ACKNOWLEDGEMENTS

PREFACE

'You should write a book.'

Mark, one of my closest Christian friends, made this pro-
nouncement as we shared a pizza together one evening in my
church flat in London. I nearly choked with laughter on a
piece of pepperoni.

That was back in the 1990s. So, as you can see, I took some
persuading before I agreed to write. But a seed had been
planted, even though it took nearly twenty years of gentle
watering and nurturing to grow.

When IVP first approached me to write this book, I was still
reluctant and hesitant, for a variety of reasons, and duly made
my excuses. Although I did sense this might be from God, so I
agreed to 'pray about it' (which seemed like a good Christian
response), I secretly hoped that praying about it would be rather
like when the government orders an enquiry into something
or sets up a commission. The issue is batted away into the long
grass and forgotten about for years. Job done – almost.

But not so. To my surprise, over the coming months God
actively dismantled my objections one by one and turned me

into a willing and eager writer. I had no time, so he moved the trustees of True Freedom Trust to kindly agree to a sabbatical. I was convinced that writing would be too lonely and discouraging, so he provided Rob Wood as a gospel partner to write with me and help guard my sanity (although, as it turned out, I had to guard his!). I felt that too many books were being published on the same-sex issue, so God convinced me I could 'add value' by writing from a somewhat different angle.

So what is that angle? Well, first this book is written by two Christians who have each been previously involved in gay relationships. (Although often written in the first-person singular, it is very much a joint enterprise.) Secondly, our different ages (at the time of writing I'm in my forties and Rob is in his twenties) help to bring two different perspectives. Thirdly, it's written not primarily to convince people that same-sex practice is sinful (although we do teach this in chapters 4 and 6). Rather, our aim is to encourage, inspire and equip Christians who struggle with same-sex temptations to make Jesus Christ their greatest treasure and live life to the full. This means that the title is indeed a bold claim.

We're convinced that ultimate satisfaction is found in and through a relationship with Christ, hence the title of this book. And that a life lived with same-sex temptations does not have to be a half-life, a lonely life or an impossible life. We hope and pray that, by reading this book, others will grasp and cling to those same convictions, and catch the vision of living joyfully in the midst of a difficult struggle.

We've written primarily with fellow strugglers in mind, although we believe the book will also be a useful resource for the friends, family and church leaders of those who face same-sex temptations. Or indeed, for anyone who simply wants to gain insight into what it's like for a same-sex attracted believer to hold to orthodox biblical teaching. Some of the chapters will resonate strongly with all single people, and those who support them in the wider church family.

This book falls into two parts. In the first half we will show that sticking to this orthodox view on sex and relationships is essential in a culture (and increasingly a church) where sexually 'anything goes'. This may appear to be a very narrow view, but Jesus warns us that only the narrow gate and the narrow way lead to the abundant life he promises. In part 2 we will set out some of the ways in which we can enjoy foretastes of this fullness of life in the here and now. Ways such as offering our bodies to God as a living sacrifice, enjoying intimacy with God and others, and unwrapping the gifts of singleness and marriage.

You may be tempted to skip over part 1, because you're already on the narrow road and are firmly convinced of the biblical arguments against same-sex practice. 'Living the abundant life' sounds more exciting, you might think. But we believe you'll gain much more from the second half of the book if you have the first part as your foundation. So if you do leapfrog chapter 4, for example, please come back to it as some stage. We're living in an age where we all need reminding of God's pattern for sex and relationships.

If you are looking for a detailed, step-by-step 'how to live the life' book, you may be disappointed. There are certainly plenty of practical tips and suggestions along the way, particularly in the later chapters on intimacy, singleness and marriage. But we are setting out to inspire people with great truths about our awesome God and his plans and purposes for our lives, rather than to write a practical guide. Great truths do need to be applied, of course, and lived out in the day-to-day realities of a world that increasingly affirms same-sex relationships.

With this in mind, we hope you will also glean practical wisdom from both our personal stories and the various pastoral conversations recounted.

In telling our stories (initially in chapter 1, and then threaded throughout the book), we've tried to strike a delicate balance. We wanted to be brutally honest about our failures and weaknesses, yet we did not want to glory in sin. It's our perception that there are many in the church who struggle in a whole variety of ways, and they are crying out for honesty and reality. At the same time, we wanted to show that it really is possible to live a fulfilling, satisfying, Christ-exalting life without acting on same-sex desires.

To this end, we have carefully selected those elements of our stories that we believe will most glorify Christ and demonstrate his amazing grace in the midst of human frailty. Elements, we hope, that will also encourage fellow strugglers (and their pastors, family and friends) to keep believing, proclaiming and teaching that Jesus really is enough. Sufficient to provide everything that a Christian battling with same-sex desires could ever need.

One of our biggest frustrations has been the need to constantly 'kill off the children'. Don't panic, the children here are all those brilliant ideas (or brilliant to us at least) born in the writing process, which had to be put to death brutally for lack of space. There's a sense in which so much more could have been said on some of the topics we've tackled. Topics like idolatry, identity and intimacy, to name just three (and that alliteration is coincidental). We have started to blog on satisfiedinchrist.com in order to explore some of these issues further.

There are also areas that we haven't tackled, a notable one being causation. This is not because we think it's unimportant, but rather because we primarily aimed to address the 'how can I live with this?' question rather than the 'why am I like this?' one.

It almost goes without saying that we're fully aware of the sensitivities around issues of faith and sexuality, not just in the UK but around the world. We have constantly tried to keep in mind the individual who's working through these issues personally, as we have had to do ourselves. And we fully recognize that many readers will have experienced a lot of pain and may find some of what we've written difficult to accept. Please be assured, though, that we have consistently prayed and strived for God's help to combine grace and truth as we've written. We hope we've achieved this, if not perfectly, then at least in good measure.

PART 1:
FINDING THE NARROW ROAD
TO ABUNDANT LIFE

1. CRAVING COUNTERFEIT GODS

I am the first and I am the last;
apart from me there is no God.
(Isaiah 44:6)

Back from captivity: Jonathan's story

'No need to worry,' said the headmaster in a stern yet vaguely reassuring tone. 'You'll be well looked after here.'

I was in floods of tears. I stared at the interior of the imposing wooden door, which moments earlier had creaked to a close behind my departing parents with an elegant yet terrifying thud. I was now officially a boarder (as opposed to a day-boy) and soon-to-be chorister at a cathedral school in the heart of England. The whole place reeked of discipline, tradition and floor polish.

Mum and Dad had sat me down months before to explain why they were sending me to a boarding school. I didn't fully understand their reasoning, but I knew that they loved me, so had no doubt that their decision was for the best. Right now, though, as I stood in the school entrance hall, the only thing registering within me was a profound sense of loss. More tears. The headmaster persevered in his detached attempts to comfort and reassure me, with little success. But suddenly and quite unexpectedly, he offered hope:

'This is Stuart,' he announced with a dignified and unconvincing half-smile. 'He's going to be your friend. He'll look after you. No need to worry.'

The boy appeared from nowhere, a broad grin on his face. He put an arm around me and gently hugged me. In my distress, it felt incredible: a rich infusion of warmth and love. What the headmaster couldn't have done with a thousand words, this boy did with a cheerful smile and an expression of genuine affection.

Stuart was lovely. He lived up to the headmaster's promise too and did become my friend. My very best friend. He did look after me and make me feel safe. No wonder, perhaps, that he quickly became the object of my love and affection. The first person – apart from my family – whom I loved, in so far as an eight-year-old boy can understand the concept of love. My first crush.

Sixteen years later, aged twenty-four, I was in floods of tears again. You might be thinking, 'Oh my, he cries a lot', but really I don't – and especially not in front of other people! This time I was sitting in the office of the Minister for Pastoral Care in a large church on the south coast of England. He had white hair and a face that radiated acceptance. With a disarming smile, he handed me a cup of tea.

'You look like you really need to talk,' he said, 'but before you do, would you mind if I read something to you from the Bible?'

I didn't mind at all. I was in despair and under deep conviction of sin. My life was a mess. Work colleagues had been saying I looked strange (well, stranger than usual), and urging me to see a doctor, fearing I was on the edge of a nervous breakdown. The minister read a passage that I later discovered came from the Old Testament:

'For I know the plans I have for you,' declares the LORD, 'plans
to prosper you and not to harm you, plans to give you hope
and a future. Then you will call on me and come and pray
to me, and I will listen to you. You will seek me and find me
when you seek me with all your heart. I will be found by you,'
declares the LORD, 'and will bring you back from captivity.'
(Jeremiah 29:11–14)

Those words were an arrow into my heart, particularly that last
word, 'captivity'. I'd been in a committed same-sex relationship
since the age of seventeen, when I had initially identified
inwardly that I was gay. Stuart had been the first in a long line
of schoolboy infatuations. Each one more intense than the
last, each ending in tears of frustration and disappointment,
each crushed under the weight of my expectations, and by
the intensity of my need to love and be loved. One friendship
after another ruined.

I'd finally met the boy of my dreams on holiday in
Switzerland. Jean-Luc was everything I'd ever longed for, physically and emotionally. It was as if all my childhood crushes
had been preparing me for this special moment when I was
finally to meet 'the one'. The difference this time was that he
wanted to be with me as much as I wanted to be with him. It
seemed perfect. Even the timing seemed perfect, as I'd met
him a year to the day after my father had died suddenly and
unexpectedly. I'd been angry with God. How could a God
of love snatch my dad away like that, leaving my mum, sister
and me alone?

God was coming good at last. Making up for the loss of
Dad, I convinced myself, by providing what I'd always longed
for. Making up for all the unrequited love of my school days
too. Here was a best friend and lover, someone to share my
whole life with, someone to take away that sense of aloneness

in this world. Jean-Luc was God's gift to me. And I even found plenty of Bible verses to back up my conviction.

I should have felt like a free man. We were in a loving, if somewhat volatile, relationship. I had a good job, a lovely home, and we were enjoying many of life's pleasures: foreign holidays, good food, nights out. Life should have been sorted. But it wasn't. Instead, I felt empty, dissatisfied, hopeless. What I'd craved and longed for since I was eight, and had now found, hadn't brought me freedom at all. It had led me into captivity. Captivity to sin, to a selfish life focused on my needs and desires being satisfied, a life devoid of God's presence.

Sitting there in the minister's office, it suddenly hit me. 'The one' I'd been relentlessly searching for since childhood wasn't a special friend or a perfect lover. It was God himself. He was the only one capable of giving me a genuine 'hope and a future'. He was the one I should be seeking with all my heart.

Jeremiah's prophecy, as I later discovered, was promising a time when God would bring his disobedient people back from captivity in Babylon. They were under God's judgment and expelled from their homeland, guilty of rejecting God's word and pursuing false gods who were powerless to satisfy. I too was under judgment. I too had turned my back on the one true God.

My Sunday school teachers had faithfully taught me about him. School friends, and later work colleagues, had boldly shared with me the good news of Jesus Christ, the Son of God. I had prayed a prayer, aged sixteen, and believed I'd become a Christian. But I didn't surrender my life to the lordship (or rule) of Jesus. He wasn't my number one. As I built a life with Jean-Luc, I rejected the advances of God, his unceasing attempts to win me over. My heart was set on one thing only: I wanted the special friend and the perfect relationship I'd craved since childhood.

I knew immediately that those words from Jeremiah were God's personal call to trust in Jesus Christ to forgive my relentless pursuit of counterfeit gods. I prayed another prayer. But this time I cried out to God with sincerity, feeling and passionate longing. Now I wanted Jesus Christ to be the most important person in my life. Now I was determined to set my heart and fix my gaze fully on him. Now he would be my number one, the perfect lover of my soul.

Within days I ended my same-sex relationship. Leaving Jean-Luc was my first significant act of repentance. No-one told me to do this. Despite years of trying to convince myself from the Bible that God approved of my relationship, deep down I always knew that he didn't. Jean-Luc didn't react well. Unsurprisingly really. There were sharp words – angry words mixed with blasphemy. There were tears. But it had to be done. The irresistible love of Christ for me, expressed supremely by his laying down his life for me on the cross, was driving out the idolatrous love I had for my partner.

I cried out to God with sincerity, feeling and passionate longing.

Ending my relationship, you may be surprised to know, was not the restrictive, negative experience you might have expected it to be. It was one of the most liberating, positive steps I've ever taken. And I wanted everyone to know about the freedom God had given me.

So when I arrived at work every morning, I would strategically place my pocket Bible on my desk. I had no fear of quoting from it, explaining to colleagues in considerable detail how I'd been convicted to end my gay relationship. Looking back, I can now see why people used to take the long route to get their drinks, deliberately bypassing my workspace.

Six months later I invited family, friends and colleagues to watch me being baptized. I was immersed under water to symbolize death to my old way of living, and (fortunately) came back up from the water to represent my new life in Christ. I was shocked when even my atheist boss Harry turned up. He was curious to know, I think, what force of nature had turned my life upside down. During the service we sang my favourite hymn. The fourth verse brilliantly encapsulates God's work of bringing me back from captivity on 12 May 1992:

> Long my imprisoned spirit lay,
> Fast bound in sin and nature's night;
> Thine eye diffused a quickening ray –
> I woke, the dungeon flamed with light;
> My chains fell off, my heart was free,
> I rose, went forth, and followed Thee.[1]

I was full of joy and hope that evening; it felt like a foretaste of heaven. I felt invincible – as if nothing could touch me or ever bring me down. Jesus Christ was everything to me. I wanted to know him better, to love him more deeply, to serve him more passionately.

Incredibly, I don't recall having a single lustful thought, or even thinking about sex or relationships, for at least a year. I believed that, by faith, God had set me free from captivity to sin. So I was somewhat bemused when other Christians would talk about battling with sexual temptations. 'Why are they fighting?' I'd ask myself. 'Don't they love Jesus?' Had they 'prayed the prayer' but not really meant it, just as I had done aged sixteen? Like many new believers, I was zealous for God. But in my zeal, I lacked wisdom.

I was also excited about God's plans to prosper me, his plans to give me hope and a future. What would this look like?

Presumably, I'd get married and have children (at least three, I decided, or maybe four, with biblical names of course – Daniel, Isaiah, Hannah and Phoebe). Oh, perhaps not straight away. But that was undoubtedly part of God's plan for my life. He would want to give me a wife and a family, wouldn't he?

And what about work? I was convinced from day one that I'd become a missionary, but should I hand in my notice straight away or wait a few weeks? The Christian life was so exciting. 'Oh happy day, oh happy day, when Jesus washed my sins away,' I'd often sing joyfully in the mornings – much to the annoyance of my colleagues.

I never imagined, in my carefree exuberance as a young believer, that my idea of prosperity might be quite different from the plans God had for me.

Broken cisterns: Rob's story

I gripped the handle of the car door, remembering as usual to look down for fear of catching my reflection in the glass of the window. As I sat next to Mum, she looked over and asked how I'd managed to get so much pen on my face at school yet again. It was now a common question.

To most people, I would have seemed like a typical thirteen-year-old boy. I hated maths, loved football, enjoyed being with friends, and would daydream for hours on end as I chewed on my pen. What they wouldn't have realized was that my aversion to maths was nothing in comparison to how much I hated my own appearance.

Even before hitting adolescence I never felt positive about my self-image, and would do everything possible throughout the day to avoid catching even a glimpse of myself in a mirror. When I would tentatively change for PE, I'd long to look like the other boys, who I thought were way more attractive than me. I've often wondered if my poor self-image contributed to my being painfully shy, introverted and without self-confidence.

Josh, by contrast, was ultra-confident. I felt nervous when we were paired together on the first day of secondary school, convinced that such a self-assured guy would never choose to sit next to someone like me. But my nerves soon dissipated, thanks to his warmth and friendliness. He had everything I thought I lacked, including a great body that he wasn't afraid to show off. Before long, innocent daydreams gave way to fantasy and lust, Josh being one of a few boys whom I found attractive and desired.

I didn't want to be gay, or if I was gay, then I certainly didn't want anyone to know. I tried to date a girl. But that didn't go too well. Sure, Jessica looked great, although however much I tried, I couldn't conjure up any feelings of attraction for her. Let's just say that our first date was kind of disastrous – and not only because I chose to take her to McDonald's.

I was desperate for help. How was I to reconcile my genuine faith in God with these sexual attractions that Pastor David said were an abomination? 'It's not Adam and Steve,' he shouted one Sunday. 'It's Adam and Eve.' 'Fair enough,' I thought, 'but I didn't choose to feel this way, so I can't help it if I'm attracted to Steve rather than Eve.' I knew from the Bible that it would be wrong to act on these attractions, so through-out my teenage years I pushed them to the back of my mind. I assumed this was a passing phase and that eventually I'd end up marrying a woman.

When I realized that these feelings were not going to go away any time soon, I decided the best thing I could do was pray. I prayed for God to intervene and change my sexual attractions. I thought back to a healing meeting where the sharply dressed preacher urged everyone to bring their needs to God – illnesses, financial problems, relationship issues – and by faith to claim his promises. 'You just have to believe,' he insisted, 'and God will grant your request.' Well, I was convinced that God was all-powerful. So, surely if I had enough faith, I would become straight. But no matter how fervently I prayed, my attractions didn't change. I didn't become straight.

I couldn't understand why God wasn't answering my prayers, and eventually I got frustrated and discouraged. Before long I was drawn into an ungodly cycle of watching porn and chatting on dating websites. After years of resisting, in my early twenties I finally gave in to the temptation to meet someone I'd been talking with online. This led to a few sexual encounters. The more attractive the man, the more I wanted affirmation through knowing that they desired me. It was a drug.

After the first sexual encounter I was consumed with guilt. I also received some shocking news. I'd been suffering from painful joints for some time, and finally got an unexpected diagnosis. I had rheumatoid arthritis. I was only twenty-one years old. 'Is God judging me?' I asked myself.

In the midst of the turmoil and questions, God challenged me with this verse from the Old Testament:

My people have committed two sins:
They have forsaken me,
    the spring of living water,
and have dug their own cisterns,
    broken cisterns that cannot hold water.
(Jeremiah 2:13)

In desperation I contacted True Freedom Trust, a Christian ministry that supports people who struggle with same-sex temptations. I needed answers; I needed hope; I needed reassurance. (Hmm, does that make me sound really needy?) I was so encouraged to receive a warm and affirming reply. But if I thought they were going to 'fix me' and make me straight, I had another think coming.

★ ★ ★

Two stories, one hero. Two journeys, one destination. Two sinners rescued by one Saviour and united by a shared vision to live the fullness of life promised by Jesus.

The twists and turns of our personal stories may surprise you. But the one who delights to prosper and not to harm is also a consuming fire, who demands to be number one in our lives.

2. MANUFACTURING IDOLS

The heart is deceitful above all things
and beyond cure.
Who can understand it?
(Jeremiah 17:9)

Mud pies in a slum

What do I first think of when I wake up?

What does my mind drift towards when it slips into neutral?

What preoccupies my thoughts most regularly?

Here's the deal. I'm not going to share my answers, and you don't have to share yours. But it's worth asking ourselves these important, if frankly uncomfortable, questions, because they help to uncover our personal idols.

By nature we all crave counterfeit gods. Idol worship might conjure up a picture of people kneeling in adoration before physical images and objects. But someone whom I love can also be an idol, or my heart can bow down to 'things'. Things such as money, sex and power. In fact, an idol is simply anyone or anything that I allow to take God's rightful place on the throne of my heart.

The greatest commandment, Jesus said, is to 'love the Lord your God with all your heart and with all your soul and with all your mind' (Matthew 22:37). Now in biblical thinking the heart is not the organ circulating blood around my body, but the command and control centre of my entire inner life. My heart relentlessly pumps out emotions, feelings and desires. Therefore the person or thing that dominates and controls the affections of my heart runs my life.

The really bad news, according to theologian John Calvin, is that the human heart is a 'perpetual factory of idols'.[1] If I'm attributing ultimate value to anyone or anything other than to the one true God, then that's an idol. Or whatever occupies my thoughts and keeps me from loving God with all my heart, soul and mind is an idol. As a boy, I idolized the desire for a special friend and the ultimate relationship. Rob craved the perfect image and affirmation through sexual encounters. (You'll have gathered that from our stories.) But possessions, hobbies, social status, career, family and even personal morality can be idols too.

Yet the foolishness of worshipping anything other than the one true God is encapsulated by C. S. Lewis in this powerful image of contrasts:

> We are half-hearted creatures, fooling about with drink and sex and ambition when infinite joy is offered us, like an ignorant child who wants to go on making mud pies in a slum because he cannot imagine what is meant by the offer of a holiday at the sea. We are far too easily pleased.[2]

Back at square one?

I'd been a Christian for just over a year. Life was wonderful. But then things changed. The best way I can describe it is that the cotton wool was removed; I was no longer a new-born Christian. God wanted to teach me to walk. This meant learning to war against sin, working out how to deal with failure, understanding and accepting his forgiveness whenever I gave in to temptation – which I'm afraid I did all too often.

The positive spin-off was that I was no longer bemused as to how Christians could struggle with sexual temptations. Now I was one of those Christians myself. My super-spiritual days of believing I'd attained sinless perfection were well and truly over, and I was learning that being tempted was part of the normal Christian life.

Keeping God as number one on the throne of my heart now became a constant challenge. But he graciously gave me some close friends to help keep me from returning to the life he'd rescued me from. Yet I had an unfortunate tendency to worship the gift, rather than the Giver of every good and perfect gift. I would sometimes become too emotionally dependent on a Christian brother. I also had a tendency to be possessive, manipulative and controlling with friends. It felt like being back at square one. I'd given up the idol of a gay relationship, but was still idolizing the perfect friendship.

I want to be like God

As a boy, I didn't get why Adam and Eve weren't allowed to eat the rosy red apple depicted in my children's Bible. It seemed like a silly, arbitrary law that didn't make sense. Why would God decide that apples were evil and all other fruits good? But soon after becoming a Christian, I made a fascinating discovery. The original sin account in Genesis 3 doesn't even mention an apple. Or a banana. Or a kiwi fruit. Or indeed any other fruit by name. Because the titanic tussle in the garden wasn't over Adam and Eve's stomachs. No, it was a battle for their eyes and their hearts.

To get at the root cause of idolatry, let's take a short trip to the Garden of Eden.

God warns Adam in Genesis 2:17 not to eat of the tree of the knowledge of good and evil, or he will surely die. The serpent directly contradicts this warning with a blatant lie to Eve: 'You will not certainly die' (Genesis 3:4). He then raises doubts in Adam and Eve's minds as to the goodness and trustworthiness of God. They're tempted to believe a lie, that God is denying them something good. The serpent is urging them to reach out and grasp at being 'like God, knowing good and evil' (Genesis 3:5).

In believing the serpent, Adam and Eve reject the truth that God is good and can be trusted as the perfect lawmaker who alone defines good and evil. They believe the lie that God is withholding something good, pleasing and desirable from them (Genesis 3:6). The irony is that they already had full access to every good thing they needed in the garden, including the tree of life.

Today the whole human race languishes under the impact of this cosmic rebellion, known as 'the fall'. You and I also want to be like God. The essence of sin is not simply that we want to *break* the rules. No, the nature of our rebellion is far more serious: we want to *make* the rules, to decide for ourselves what's good and what's evil, rather than submit to the infinite wisdom of our Maker.

We can see this in people's attitudes towards sex and relationships. The idea of a supreme being telling me what I can or cannot do in the privacy of my own bedroom is simply abhorrent to many. Everyone wants to decide for themselves what's morally right. If a sexual relationship makes me happy and I'm not harming anyone else, then what's the problem?

Poor exchange rate

This desire to be like God, inherited from our ancestors, helps us to see why our hearts tend to worship idols rather than the one true God. We've 'exchanged the truth about God for a lie, and worshipped and served created things rather than the Creator', explains the apostle Paul in Romans 1:25. In rejecting the truth about God and failing to worship him with our whole being, we have nowhere else to turn except to ourselves or other created things.

So today people worship and serve pornographic images, and it's no surprise that globally porn is a $97 billion industry.[3] If pornography is an issue in your life, you may never have thought of it as idol worship. But that's exactly what it is. Speaking personally, I've had several seasons of struggling with pornography as a Christian. And it's challenging to think that instead of worshipping and serving my Creator, I've been bowing down to, and lusting over, naked, sexual images of people he's created in his image.

Nothing in this world, no matter how beautiful and wonderful, can ever match the glorious splendour of our Creator.

It doesn't matter what or who we choose to replace God with, it will always be a poor exchange. Nothing in this world, no matter how beautiful and wonderful, can ever match the glorious splendour of our Creator.

God goes public

So the essence of idolatry is that we exchange the glory of God for counterfeit gods which are unable to satisfy the deepest longings of our hearts. But what exactly is the glory of God? Author and preacher John Piper contrasts God's glory with his holiness, which he suggests is God being in a class by himself in his perfection, greatness and worth. Piper then attempts a definition of God's glory as 'the manifest beauty of his holiness. It is the going public of his holiness. It is the way he puts his holiness on display for people to apprehend.'[4]

In response to Moses' bold request in the Old Testament to see God's glory, God makes all his goodness pass before him and proclaims his name:

> The LORD, the LORD, the compassionate and gracious God,
> slow to anger, abounding in love and faithfulness, maintaining
> love to thousands, and forgiving wickedness, rebellion and sin.
> Yet he does not leave the guilty unpunished.
> (Exodus 34:6–7)

With such an immense revelation of the glory of the one true God, why would anyone ever want to exchange his glory for idols? Idols that cannot begin to match the supreme goodness of God, and cannot forgive our wickedness, rebellion and sin? Why do we all naturally seek satisfaction apart from God's glory? Well, the inevitable outcome of suppressing the truth about God, according to Romans 1, is that I become a fool: 'Although they claimed to be wise, they became fools and exchanged the glory of the immortal God for images made to look like a mortal human being and birds and animals and reptiles' (Romans 1:22–23).

Athanasius of Alexandria summed it up like this in the fourth century:

> Men, foolish as they are, thought little of the grace they had received, and turned away from God. They defiled their own soul so completely that they not only lost their apprehension of God, but invented for themselves other gods of various kinds.[5]

Glorious exchange

Many same-sex attracted Christians have one great fear: if we obey Jesus and say no to the idol of an immoral relationship, aren't we consigning ourselves to a life of sadness, loneliness and frustration?

By denying himself a same-sex relationship, Amir, a friend of mine, worries that he may be missing out on an opportunity for happiness: 'I don't want to reach old age and be full of regrets, to wonder what it would have been like to have fallen in love and shared my life with someone special.'

But Jesus came so that we 'may have life, and have it to the full' (John 10:10). That sounds to me like Jesus is promising his followers a truly satisfying life, rather than setting us up for future regrets and disappointment. But the strange paradox of this fullness of life is that I can only experience it by being willing to lose my own version of life, which will always be a poor imitation of the real thing:

> Whoever wants to be my disciple must deny themselves and take up their cross and follow me. For whoever wants to save their life will lose it, but whoever loses their life for me and for the gospel will save it. What good is it for someone to gain the whole world, yet forfeit their soul?
>
> (Mark 8:34–36)

But Jesus understands the immense cost of self-denial. I find that hugely reassuring. He lost his life in obedience to his Father and for the sake of the gospel. In the Garden of Eden, Adam and Eve ate from the tree of the knowledge of good and evil; in rebellion they grasped at the opportunity to become like God. Yet in the Garden of Gethsemane, Jesus didn't consider equality with God something to cling to, but willingly took up the tree of his crucifixion.

Adam and Eve disobeyed God. By contrast, Jesus, though he cried out in anguish, 'Take this cup from me', denied himself and obediently submitted to his Father, saying, 'Yet not my will, but yours be done' (Luke 22:42). Amazingly, Jesus exchanged the glory of heaven for servanthood. Through his death on the cross in our place and on our behalf, he rescues us from our foolish idolatry and reconciles us to God:

> Christ Jesus, who, though he was in the form of God, did not count equality with God a thing to be grasped, but emptied himself, by taking the form of a servant, being born in the likeness of men. And being found in human form, he humbled himself by becoming obedient to the point of death, even death on a cross.
> (Philippians 2:5–8 ESV)

So God sent his very own Son to empty himself so that you and I can experience life to the full. Such a glorious exchange demands a very serious response from those of us who call ourselves disciples of Jesus.

Radical heart surgery

People often ask me for pastoral advice about dealing with their personal idols – not that I ever set myself up as an expert, although I've definitely had plenty of experience of trying to root out my own. Questions include: 'How do I handle a friendship that's become too intense and all-consuming?', 'Should I get rid of my laptop if pornography is a snare?' and 'Would it be best to give up my gym membership if I can't stop myself from lusting in the changing rooms?'

If we recognize that someone or something is taking God's place as the 'ultimate' in our heart, or impeding our worship of God, then we need to consider radical action. I find it helpful to view these things under one of three categories.

Some are clearly *ungodly* according to God's word, and simply need to be removed from our lives: a sexually immoral relationship, for example, or sexually explicit material.

Other things are *neutral*: a media device such as a TV, tablet or smartphone, or perhaps a social media profile, or instant / video messaging apps. Each one can potentially be used either for good or for evil. So social media can be an effective way of staying in touch with your friends (Rob assures me), or a source of temptation if someone attractive posts photos that cause you to lust. A gym membership can be a good means of staying fit and looking after the body God has given you, or a constant means of stumbling.

Things in the neutral category may need to be removed from our lives if they regularly cause us to fall into sin. Rob ditched his smartphone, as he was finding certain apps to be a constant source of temptation. He now gets strange looks when he pulls out his uncool 'brick' phone. But he finds this shame a price worth paying, as the lack of a smartphone helps him to steer clear of unhelpful material. This kind of radical action might not always be necessary, for sometimes we can learn to exercise self-control by the power of the Holy Spirit so that the neutral thing in question is used only for godly purposes.

The third category is: things that are *intrinsically good*. These are gifts from God. But gifts that have become more important to me than my relationship with him. So a vocation maybe, a home, an area of Christian service, my body, a friend, a spouse, or even my children. If any of these good gifts has become an object of worship, it will need to be prayerfully devoted back to God as the Giver of that gift.

When I have idolized a friend, prayerfully involving God in the struggle has been the only way to break the power of that idol. God already knows what's in my heart, but he delights in his children being completely real with him in prayer. I have often prayed something like: 'Lord, this person belongs to you, not to me. Help me to love them, but to worship you alone. Help me to keep you at the centre of my life as my undisputed number one.'

The poet and hymnwriter expressed it well:

The dearest idol I have known,
Whate'er that idol be,
Help me to tear it from thy throne,
And worship only thee.[6]

Tearing idols from our heart can be a very painful process. But what if we fail to take the radical action needed? Will God just let the matter lie? His response may not be quite what we expect.

3. A JEALOUS GOD – AND SECOND CHANCES

For the LORD *your God is a consuming fire, a jealous God.*
(Deuteronomy 4:24)

Green eyes

One Sunday after the morning service I was longing to catch up with my new friend Ben. I'd had a really stressful week at work, albeit self-inflicted. I still lacked wisdom as a young believer, and probably shouldn't have changed the screensavers on all the office computers to show John 3:16. Anyway, I knew Ben would offer helpful words of encouragement.

'Sorry, Jonathan, I'm in a hurry, meeting my friend Andrew for lunch. Do you mind if we catch up sometime next week?'

I'd met Ben in the 18–30s group at church. He stood out from the crowd. Not only because he was good-looking, but also because he seemed somewhat on the fringe – as if he didn't quite fit in. He was also really shy and lacked confidence. For all these reasons, I was drawn to him. I wanted to get to know him. I wanted to be his best friend.

We started to spend time together and quickly clicked. We spent more time together. It didn't take long before I felt comfortable enough to tell Ben about my past life and my on-going same-sex temptations. He wasn't fazed at all. He assured me this revelation wouldn't affect our friendship negatively, and he was true to his word: if anything, we grew even closer.

But with the deepening friendship came growing insecurity. It was reminiscent of my relationship with Jean-Luc. I'd worshipped Jean-Luc. He was my life. Whenever I perceived any threat to our relationship, that fuelled my fear of losing him. I'd loved him with all my heart, and at times I'd become really jealous.

'No, of course, Ben. That's fine. I don't mind at all.'

My heart sank. And I did mind. 'Who is this Andrew?' I thought. 'Ben's never mentioned him before. Why doesn't he just cancel his plans?' I burned with jealousy.

The God named Jealous

Jealousy is commonly seen as an emotion that does more harm than good. 'Never underestimate the power of jealousy and the power of envy to destroy,'[1] said film director Oliver Stone. Wary of jealousy's reputation for destruction, Iago warns his old friend Othello in Shakespeare's play, 'Beware, my lord, of jealousy; it is the green-eyed monster.'[2]

If you've ever felt the force of a jealous outburst, you may find this command in Exodus 34:14 unsettling, disturbing even: 'Do not worship any other god, for the LORD, whose name is Jealous, is a jealous God.'

But God is not tainted by negative connotations of human jealousy; he doesn't fly off the handle in a fit of rage whenever his people stray by worshipping idols. No, God is consistently jealous. His name is Jealous.

TV host Oprah Winfrey turned away from authentic biblical Christianity in her late twenties when her Baptist minister preached about God's jealousy. 'God is jealous of me?' the American media icon said on her talk show. 'Something about that didn't feel right in my spirit because I believe that God is love.'[3] Oprah thinks, as many do, that God cannot be both jealous and loving.

But jealousy and love are entirely compatible where God is concerned. Surprising as it may sound, jealousy is a positive, loving attribute, essential to the divine nature. God is jealous for his people because he knows that he alone is worthy of our worship and adoration. Competitors for our worship cannot be tolerated, because even the 'best' idol will be an inadequate substitute for our perfect Creator, and for this reason they can never ultimately satisfy us. 'Man's chief end is to glorify God and to enjoy him forever',[4] according to the Westminster Shorter Catechism.

New life, new love

Yet the God named Jealous is amazingly gracious. He is well within his rights, as our sovereign Creator, simply to demand and insist on the worship and devotion of his creatures – he doesn't even need to explain himself. But despite this, he lovingly chooses to reveal the fundamental reason why he merits the undivided worship of our hearts. The first of the Ten Commandments, forbidding the worship of other gods, is rooted in God's magnificent act of redemption (rescue by payment of a ransom):

> I am the LORD your God, who brought
> you out of Egypt, out of the land
> of slavery.
> You shall have no other gods before me.
> (Exodus 20:2–3)

So God's people are not to have any other gods before the Lord, because he alone is the great Redeemer who sets his people free. The Israelites were delivered from slavery in Egypt and brought into the Promised Land of Canaan. Similarly, and more significantly, Christians are rescued from slavery to sin in the dominion of darkness and brought into the kingdom of the Son God loves (Colossians 1:13).

For us to be rescued from our enslavement to sin and brought into the kingdom (or under the rule) of Jesus Christ, a ransom had to be paid. 'Without the shedding of blood,' says the writer of Hebrews, 'there is no forgiveness' (Hebrews 9:22). And the glory of the gospel is that Jesus' blood was shed. As we saw in the last chapter, that's the ransom price. His life in exchange for mine. His death in my place, paying for my sins. Amazing!

Having demonstrated the extent of his love by sacrificing what was most precious to him, it's no surprise that God now commands his people to 'have no other gods before me'. Surely he merits our undivided devotion and obedience? And not slavish obedience either. Instead, our response should be one of gratitude and love.

God's treasured possession

'I flushed it down the toilet. It's gone.'

Three-year-old Munazzar Tapal had somehow got his hands on his mother's diamond and sapphire ring. Apparently inspired by watching the film *Finding Nemo*, he flushed the priceless heirloom, passed down from Munazzar's great-grandfather, down the loo. After frantic attempts by plumbers to find the ring, the family realized it was lost in the vast Californian sewer system. But incredibly, sanitation workers managed to find it – more than a third of a mile from the family home.[5]

I imagine that the Tapal family learnt a valuable lesson. Family heirlooms should not be entrusted to lively three-year-olds with adventurous minds. They should be wrapped up carefully and stored it in a safe, secure place. They need to be protected, guarded, treasured.

We can rest assured that God is not careless when it comes to looking after his redeemed people. Quite the opposite. He zealously guards those whom he has rescued as if they were the most precious gemstones imaginable: 'For you are a people holy to the LORD your God. The LORD your God has chosen you out of all the peoples on the face of the earth to be his people, his treasured possession' (Deuteronomy 7:6).

Isn't that amazing? You might wonder if that Old Testament verse has any relevance to Christians today. Absolutely! If you're trusting in Jesus Christ, then you're included in God's treasure trove, precious and immeasurably valuable in his sight:

> But you are a chosen people, a royal priesthood, a holy nation, God's special possession, that you may declare the praises of him who called you out of darkness into his wonderful light. Once you were not a people, but now you are the people of God; once you had not received mercy, but now you have received mercy.
> (1 Peter 2:9–10)

Second chances?

'Men cheat more as age milestones approach' ran the headline in *The Times*, above a report analysing 8 million male users on a website for extramarital dating. And men are more likely to be unfaithful in the year leading up to milestone birthdays such as thirty, forty, fifty and sixty, researchers claimed. Data from women using the site suggested a similar trend, although not nearly as strong as for men.[6]

Infidelity in marriage is one sad and awful consequence of humankind's rebellious, sinful nature. Unfaithfulness can lead, among other things, to immense pain and heartache, to a complete breakdown in trust, to bitterness and, ultimately of course, to the tragic sorrow of divorce.

So it may surprise you that God uses a powerful story of infidelity to illustrate his unceasing love for his spiritually adulterous people. God instructs his prophet Hosea: 'Go, marry a promiscuous woman and have children with her, for like an adulterous wife this land is guilty of unfaithfulness to the LORD' (Hosea 1:2).

Don't you find that shocking? I do. God, the Holy One, commands his holy prophet to take a promiscuous woman to be his lawfully wedded wife. Yes, you read that correctly. Hosea obeys God, despite the shame of such a union, and marries unfaithful Gomer. They have children together, but, unsurprisingly perhaps, Gomer leaves him and returns to her old ways. God later gives Hosea an instruction that is no less astounding, one that would surely fly in the face of how many would react today if confronted with a consistently cheating spouse: 'Go, show your love to your wife again, though she is loved by another man and is an adulteress. Love her as the LORD loves the Israelites, though they turn to other gods' (Hosea 3:1).

Hosea again obeys and remains faithful to his wife. As if the shame of the original marriage to Gomer wasn't enough, he now pays the required price to redeem her and bring her back home. You can imagine the neighbours peeking from behind their curtains with disapproving looks, or the warnings and urgent relationship advice from Hosea's concerned friends.

But God uses this account to illustrate his great faithfulness to his treasured possession, Israel, even in the face of their persistent spiritual adultery and unfaithfulness. By turning to other gods, they deserve God's judgment. This is duly pronounced through the naming of Hosea and Gomer's children. When their daughter is born, God says, 'Call her Lo-Ruhamah (which means "not loved"), for I will no longer show love to Israel, that I should at all forgive them' (Hosea 1:6). Then at the birth of their second son, God says, 'Call him Lo-Ammi (which means "not my people"), for you are not my people, and I am not your God' (Hosea 1:9).

The Lord, though, demonstrates a zealous and unceasing love for his rebellious people and will not reject them forever. Just as he told Hosea to take back unfaithful Gomer, so the God of all love and faithfulness promises future restoration to Israel:

> I will plant her for myself in the land;
>> I will show my love to the one I called
>>> 'Not my loved one'.
> I will say to those called 'Not my people',
>> 'You are my people';
>> and they will say, 'You are my God.'
> (Hosea 2:23)

This unlikely love affair reveals to us the God who, though provoked to jealousy, pursues his rebellious people in mercy, even as he exercises fatherly discipline. The God of all grace and compassion simply will not abandon the relentless pursuit of his people:

> How can I give you up . . . ?
> My heart is changed within me;
>> all my compassion is aroused.

I will not carry out my fierce anger ...
For I am God, and not a man –
   the Holy One among you.
(Hosea 11:8–9)

Lost, found and celebrated

Have you ever felt that God has given up on you? That perhaps you've provoked the God named Jealous just once too often? Maybe you've become enslaved to a particular pattern of sinful behaviour. Or there may be one serious failure for which you're struggling to receive God's forgiveness. Or you might accept that God has forgiven you for past offences, but believe you're no longer useful to him as damaged goods.

But however far you may have strayed from God's word, you can be confident that Hosea's God has not changed. Even today the God whose 'compassion is aroused' is not in the business of abandoning his chosen people. To my shame, I have a tendency sometimes to give up on people far too quickly. But God's not like that; he is God and not a human.

Before Rob started volunteering with True Freedom Trust he was concerned that his lack of a perfect record as a Christian in the area of sexual purity might exclude him from serving God. It has been a joy to witness the transformation in his outlook as he's come to learn and experience that God is pleased to use even imperfect people in his service. As we will see later, it is in weakness that God's power is made perfect. The fact that Rob has not lived a faultless life, and knows what it is to be pursued by a jealous God, enables him to relate well to others struggling with same-sex desires.

As for me, I'd love to claim that I have lived a perfect life of sexual purity and celibacy since becoming a Christian. As you know, the reality is that I haven't. As a result, I have sometimes had to experience God's loving, fatherly hand of discipline.

But the Lord has never given up on me. He has consistently pursued me in love. When I've strayed from his truth, the Holy Spirit has always convicted me, led me to repentance and steered me back onto the narrow path which Jesus assures us leads to life. I've come to better understand and experience, through these struggles, the amazing grace of the Great Shepherd who simply will not abandon his wayward sheep:

I've come to better understand and experience . . . the amazing grace of the Great Shepherd who simply will not abandon his wayward sheep.

> Suppose one of you has a hundred sheep and loses one of them. Doesn't he leave the ninety-nine in the open country and go after the lost sheep until he finds it? And when he finds it, he joyfully puts it on his shoulders and goes home. Then he calls his friends and neighbours together and says, 'Rejoice with me; I have found my lost sheep.' I tell you that in the same way there will be more rejoicing in heaven over one sinner who repents than over ninety-nine righteous people who do not need to repent.
> (Luke 15:4–7)

I wonder if you've ever thought about that before? When you or I repent (have a change of mind that leads to a change in the way we live), this causes great celebrations in heaven. When we respond to the loving advances of our jealous God by turning back and making Jesus number one, this is certainly good news for us. But more importantly, it also brings great honour to him, because, as John Piper puts it, 'God is most glorified in us when we are most satisfied in him.'[7] No wonder the angels in heaven throw a party!

Is it not possible, though, to be fully satisfied in him while at the same time enjoying a loving, monogamous same-sex relationship? God is love, after all. So, as long as God remains number one, and as long as I don't provoke his jealousy by loving someone else *more* than I love him, then surely he wouldn't deny me a loving same-sex partnership? Or would he?

4. DID GOD REALLY SAY . . . ?

The time will come when people will not put up with
sound doctrine. Instead, to suit their own desires,
they will gather round them a great number of teachers
to say what their itching ears want to hear.
(2 Timothy 4:3)

Modern Family

The US comedy *Modern Family* portrays three interrelated families, including Mitch and Cam, who've celebrated a same-sex marriage ceremony and adopted a girl from Vietnam.

The title intrigues me. I don't know what the producers had in mind, but *Modern Family* appears to challenge those who hold to a 'traditional' view of family. The implication is that anyone who doesn't embrace this 'modern' concept of same-sex marriage is out-dated, old-fashioned and, frankly, out of touch.

This TV show reflects the dramatic shift in attitudes to same-sex relationships. When US actor and TV host Ellen DeGeneres came out as gay on the cover of *Time* magazine in 1997, this caused quite a stir.[1] But when singer-songwriter Sam Smith came out in 2014, he revealed that his first album

In the Lonely Hour was inspired by a man he loved, and asserted, 'It's as normal as my right arm.'[2] In less than twenty years the shock value of a celebrity coming out had diminished to virtually zero. Today it's just plain normal.

This cultural tsunami of popular support for same-sex relationships has led to increased confusion in the church over their legitimacy. Christians are under great pressure to 'catch up' with society and affirm same-sex unions. Those who hold to the orthodox biblical view of sex and relationships, even if they do so with grace and love, are often branded as intolerant and homophobic.

With all this in mind, it's no surprise that a growing number of Christians are asking, 'Does God really say no to same-sex relationships?'

Divine spoilsport?

To understand the origins of this question, let's return to the Garden of Eden. We saw earlier how the serpent contradicted God and planted doubt in the minds of Adam and Eve as to their Creator's integrity and motives. His primary strategy, as he sought to lead them astray, was to sow confusion about both the reliability and the content of God's word: 'Now the snake was more crafty than any of the wild animals the LORD God had made. He said to the woman, "Did God really say, 'You must not eat from any tree in the garden'?"' (Genesis 3:1).

This is very crafty indeed. Just one question, but within it two major attacks on God's word. First, he questions its reliability: 'Did God *really* say . . . ?' But secondly, and much more subtly, he distorts its content, because God did not say this at all. The devious serpent deliberately misquotes God and, by massively expanding the restriction, makes his command sound onerous and unfair. In doing this, he caricatures God as a divine spoilsport.

This is what God actually said: 'You are free to eat from *any* tree in the garden; but you must not eat from the tree of the knowledge of good and evil, for when you eat from it you will certainly die' (Genesis 2:16–17, italics mine).

Still today our enemy the devil prowls around like a roaring lion looking for someone to devour (1 Peter 5:8). And his tactics haven't changed. Attacking God's word continues to be a major strategy.

Satan works hard to create doubt about the Bible's reliability and to stir up confusion about its content. This has had a devastating impact on the church, not least in the area of sex and relationships. Did Jesus really say no to sex outside of marriage? Did Jesus really say that anyone who divorces his wife, except for sexual immorality, makes her the victim of adultery? Did Jesus (through his appointed messenger) really say that those who continue in same-sex practice will not inherit the kingdom of God?

Painful choice: Rob's story

'Do you want to go for a coffee?' This seemingly mundane and innocent question would become one of the most significant invitations I'd ever respond to. On that breezy spring day I headed to Costa Coffee not knowing what to expect. Some things, however, were abundantly clear. I was attracted to the same sex (but not open about it). I hadn't experienced a change in my sexual attractions. I was lonely. This was as far from 'fixed' as I ever thought I could be.

I arrived about ten minutes before Tim, who came into the coffee shop looking windswept, phone glued to his ear. He hung up as soon as he saw me, walked over and gingerly offered a handshake. Three lattes later and the conversation was still flowing. It was partly the excitement of feeling a connection, but the influence of caffeine shouldn't be underestimated either. By the end of the evening the ache of loneliness had already strangely dissipated.

Over the next few days Tim and I spent a great deal of time together and quickly grew close. It was intense. Before long I was in my first and only same-sex relationship. But there was a major problem: I still called myself a Christian and I believed that same-sex practice was incompatible with Christian discipleship. Something had to give. I didn't want to abandon my faith, but I wasn't prepared to water down the Bible's teaching either. I didn't want to commit sexual immorality, but neither was I ready to give up Tim. Was it possible to reconcile my faith with being in a loving same-sex relationship?

I started to look into the teachings of those who celebrate same-sex relationships. How did they justify this view biblically? I was desperate to find something. Was there a Bible verse promoting same-sex relationships that had perhaps gone unread for thousands of years? The answer was no. Throughout church history, had any great theological minds ever contradicted the clear and consistent teachings of God's word on same-sex practice? I looked at the writings of Athanasius, Augustine, Anselm, Luther, Calvin, Wesley, Spurgeon, Barth, C. S. Lewis, John Stott and others. But again the answer was no.

I wondered if perhaps I was misunderstanding the biblical teaching on sex and relationships. But as I read my Bible, it all seemed crystal clear to me. Sex is a good gift from God, but one to be enjoyed only within heterosexual marriage. Any other sexual practice is categorized as sexual immorality.

Now, of course, recognizing what God's word says and putting it into practice are two different things. I wasn't actually taking the Bible very seriously. Jesus had called me to take up my cross and follow him (Matthew 16:24), but I was still seeking a life outside of his teachings. I hadn't fully lost my life so that I could find it. If Jesus was who he said he was (and I still believed he was), I had to obey him in every area of my life. This inevitably meant giving up my same-sex relationship. Ouch!

Tim knew I was wrestling with reconciling my faith and my sexuality, and sensed that I wasn't fully committed to a long-term relationship. In God's providence this proved to be the catalyst for things to come to an end. Tim gave me an ultimatum. Understandably. I had to decide between loving him or following Jesus. Or I could follow Jesus if I changed my beliefs about gay relationships. It was a painful choice. But I knew there could be only one winner.

Tim didn't want things to end and was convinced that I wouldn't be happy if I denied myself a relationship. He challenged me again to reconsider my beliefs. But my mind was already made up, so I threw a challenge back to Tim. What could he offer me that was better than my relationship with Jesus? What would he be able to say on my behalf when I would come face to face with the Lord Jesus in the future and have to give an account of my life? He had no answer. Just silence.

Through this whole experience I came to realize that a same-sex relationship could never be the solution to my loneliness. This surprised me, as I'd always assumed that this would make me happy: even a counsellor at church had once urged me just to accept my sexuality and find a partner. But now I could see that the root cause of my loneliness was a failure to devote myself entirely to Jesus.

I do regret the pain I caused Tim, but, by God's grace, I've never regretted the decision to leave that relationship and follow Christ. Since turning back to God, I've started to taste something of the inexpressible joy that comes to those who believe in, and follow, Jesus Christ.

Jesus and same-sex practice: four important truths

When I (Jonathan) chat about faith and the Bible with gay friends, many comment that Jesus doesn't actually express a view on same-sex practice. Some Christians now accept such statements as fact and don't know how to counteract them. But we must counteract what's untrue. Through his teaching on sex and marriage, Jesus clearly prohibits same-sex practice. Let's look at four important truths.

Jesus teaches that:

1. *Marriage must be between one man and one woman*

When the Marriage (Same Sex Couples) Act 2013 received Royal Assent, this paved the way for the first civil same-sex marriages to take place in England and Wales. Sir Elton John subsequently converted his civil partnership to a same-sex marriage. Interviewed by *Sky News*, he said, 'If Jesus Christ was alive today, I cannot see him, as the Christian person that he was and the great person that he was, saying this could not happen.'[3]

But Jesus did say this could not happen. Some elite religious leaders once questioned him, trying to catch him out on the subject of divorce. Their knowledge of what we call the Old Testament was second to none. So it's somewhat shocking that Jesus replies, 'Haven't you read . . . ?' before quoting from Genesis. We can imagine these respected, scholarly men feeling insulted by the suggestion that they don't know their Scriptures!

'Haven't you read,' he replied, 'that at the beginning the Creator "made them male and female", [see Genesis 1:27] and said, "for

this reason a man will leave his father and mother and be
united to his wife, and the two will become one flesh"?
[see Genesis 2:24] So they are no longer two, but one flesh.
Therefore what God has joined together, let no one separate.'
(Matthew 19:4–6)

In answering their question on divorce, Jesus relies on the
authority of Scripture and outlines a clear definition of
marriage. He believes that the written word of God in Genesis
1 and 2 is clear, and must govern their (and our) thinking on
all sexual relationships.

It's worth noting here that Jesus has complete confidence
in the Old Testament Scriptures. He was evidently convinced
about their reliability and accuracy, taking them to be authoritative in all matters of faith and conduct, including sexual
relationships. He both refers to, and directly quotes from, the
creation account. And by doing so, he reinforces the unchanging creation principle that the complementarity of the sexes
is an essential, non-negotiable ingredient of marriage in
God's eyes.

Paul too recognizes the importance of this truth in Romans
1. He also draws on the creation account when he writes
about the consequences of exchanging the truth about God
for a lie. So there are several allusions to Genesis 1 and 2 in
the opening chapter of Romans, for example, in verses 20, 23
and 25–27.

One such consequence of exchanging the truth about God
for a lie is that some 'women exchanged natural sexual
relations for unnatural ones' (verse 26), and some 'men also
abandoned natural relations with women and were inflamed
with lust for one another' (verse 27). So Paul agrees with Jesus
that same-sex relationships are contrary to God's natural
created order.

But what about that objection we mentioned at the end of the previous chapter? Surely a loving God wouldn't want to deny two people of the same sex the blessing of being in a loving relationship? Well, it's certainly true that 'God is love' (1 John 4:8). But our loving God is also the perfect lawmaker. As such, he alone has the right to define the boundaries of erotic love. And God is clear in Genesis 2:24 that 'a man leaves his father and mother and is united to his wife, and they become one flesh'. So marriage in God's eyes involves a man being joined to his wife, not a man to his husband, nor a woman to her wife.

But our loving God is also the perfect lawmaker.

By reiterating and restating this truth in the Gospels, Jesus makes it plain that he has not redefined marriage. This verse is like a thread that runs throughout the whole Bible, from Genesis to Revelation. All biblical teaching on sex and relationships is built upon, and flows from, the unchanging foundation of Genesis 2:24.

2. All sex outside of marriage is sexual immorality

My relationship with Jean-Luc was very loving, and we were deeply committed to one another. We didn't sleep around and, to my knowledge, we didn't harm anyone else. The same was true of Rob's relationship with Tim. But this doesn't change the fact that, according to Jesus, both relationships were sexually immoral.

On one occasion the Pharisees quiz Jesus as to why his disciples are 'eating their food with defiled [unwashed] hands' (Mark 7:5). He responds by giving them a lesson in true defilement:

What comes out of a person is what defiles them. For it is
from within, out of a person's heart, that evil thoughts come
– sexual immorality, theft, murder, adultery, greed, malice,
deceit, lewdness, envy, slander, arrogance and folly. All these
evils come from inside and defile a person.
(Mark 7:20–23)

The term 'sexual immorality' is translated from the Greek
word *porneiai* (plural). This carries the meaning of all sexual
activity outside of marriage (as defined in Genesis 2:24), so
it's an all-inclusive term. When Jesus spoke these words, his
Jewish listeners would have had in mind the various pro-
hibited sexual acts outlined in Leviticus 18 and 20, including
same-sex practice. Jesus doesn't explicitly name all sexual sins;
rather, he uses the catch-all word *porneiai*.

The implication of this teaching in Mark 7 is that all of us
have in our hearts the capacity to commit sexual immorality.
For most, the temptation is to have illicit sex with someone of
the opposite sex. For some, however, it's to have illicit sex with
those of the same sex. Whatever our particular temptation,
Jesus reiterates the truth that God intends the good gift of sex
to be enjoyed exclusively within heterosexual marriage, and
any other sexual relationship, same sex or opposite sex, is sinful.

3. He (Jesus) has not abolished the Old Testament laws on sexual morality

People who argue for acceptance of same-sex relationships
in the church will sometimes claim (incorrectly) that it's
mainly the Old Testament that speaks so negatively about it.
And they say this as if Jesus somehow has no connection with
the Old Testament. But Jesus, of course, is the divine author
of the Old Testament; he is the Word become flesh. Let's hear
what Jesus has to say about the Old Testament Scriptures:

> Do not think that I have come to abolish the Law or the
> Prophets; I have not come to abolish them but to fulfil
> them. For truly I tell you, until heaven and earth disappear,
> not the smallest letter, not the least stroke of a pen, will
> by any means disappear from the Law until everything is
> accomplished.
> (Matthew 5:17–18)

Could Jesus be clearer? He did not come to abolish even one letter of the Old Testament Scriptures, but came instead to fulfil (or complete) them. So he hasn't abolished Leviticus 18:22, for example, which says, 'Do not have sexual relations with a man as one does with a woman; that is detestable.' It must be stressed, of course, that Leviticus 18 also forbids a whole host of other immoral sexual relations.

At this stage many people, including my biblically astute gay friend Liam, raise an objection: 'Why do you obey certain Old Testament laws, but not others?'

It's an excellent question. In his light-hearted and at times irreverent book, *The Year of Living Biblically*,[4] A. J. Jacobs demonstrates how difficult it is to live today according to all the laws of Moses. Pinning tassels onto his shirt-sleeves to ensure he doesn't fall foul of Numbers 15:38 seems easy enough. But his wife finds it distracting – and probably embarassing – when, in an attempt to obey Leviticus 19:32, he stands up whenever an older man enters a restaurant.

Confession is good for the soul, as the saying goes. So here are three confessions from me:

- I have never yet sacrificed a sheep, goat or pigeon before a church service. But the Law demands an animal sacrifice to atone for sin.

- I have a polycotton shirt lurking somewhere in my wardrobe. But Deuteronomy 22:11 outlaws wearing clothes made of mixed fibres.
- I'm partial to the occasional packet of prawn cocktail crisps. But the Old Testament forbids the eating of shellfish.

So why do I ignore those laws, yet believe that same-sex relationships are sinful? Jesus helps to unlock the answer in that quote above from the Sermon on the Mount. He came to 'fulfil' the Law, or to complete it. And nothing will 'disappear from the Law until everything is accomplished'. Surely then I have to ask, which laws has Jesus already fulfilled or accomplished? Or are there any laws on which Jesus gives some specific direction?

Let's try applying those questions to my three confessions:

Animal sacrifices

Has Jesus abolished the laws about making animal sacrifices? Absolutely not! But he *has* fulfilled them. To be more precise, Jesus, the Lamb of God, *is* the fulfilment of them. Christ 'was sacrificed once to take away the sins of many' (Hebrews 9:28). The sacrificial laws were always just a shadow of the good things to come, but it is impossible for the blood of bulls and goats to take away sins (Hebrews 10:1, 4). Christians, then, no longer need to offer sacrifices for our sins.

Clothing

Should I suffer sleepless nights over that polycotton shirt? I've thought about giving it away to a charity shop, but what if another Christian buys it? Quite apart from the fashion faux pas, I'd hate to cause anybody else to stumble. But I can relax. Nowhere in the New Testament do Jesus or his apostles teach that refraining from wearing clothes made of mixed fibres is a mark of Christian holiness.

Food

And can I eat my prawn cocktail crisps with a clear conscience? Happily, Jesus teaches that it's not what we eat or drink that makes us 'unclean', but rather what's already in our hearts, the implication being that Christians can eat all foods with a clear conscience because Jesus has declared them clean (Mark 7:19). The apostle Peter receives the same message when, in a vision, a voice from heaven commands him to kill and eat food that was forbidden in the Old Testament (Acts 10:9–16).

But there's no similar 'release clause' for sexual relationships forbidden in the Old Testament. Jesus and his apostles do not declare all sexual relationships as now 'clean' (that is, holy and acceptable to God). On the contrary, in the New Testament, as we'll see shortly, Christians are clearly taught to flee from sexual immorality (*porneia*). We're to avoid it, not to allow even a hint of it in our lives.

4. Believers are to have a different sexual ethic from that of our culture

Those who take a different view on same-sex relationships (sometimes called a 'revisionist' view) will often point to the need to understand the cultural and historical context of specific passages that forbid same-sex practice. And I completely agree.

With this in mind, let's consider Leviticus 18:22. It's that Old Testament verse mentioned a few pages back that prohibits male-to-male same-sex practice, and which, remember, Jesus has not abolished. The opening verses of chapter 18 explain the context:

The LORD said to Moses, 'Speak to the Israelites and say to them: "I am the LORD your God. You must not do as they do in Egypt, where you used to live, and you must not do as they do in the land of Canaan, where I am bringing you. Do not follow their practices. You must obey my laws and be careful to follow my decrees. I am the LORD your God. Keep my decrees and laws, for the person who obeys them will live by them. I am the LORD."'
(Leviticus 18:1–5)

So the context of Leviticus 18:22 is clear. God's redeemed people – rescued out of Egypt in the case of the Israelites, and out of the dominion of darkness in the case of Christians – are to have a distinctively different sexual ethic from that of the surrounding culture: 'You shall not do as they do . . . Do not follow their practices. You must obey my laws and be careful to follow my decrees.' God's people are called to stand out from the culture in our sexual behaviour, rather than allow ourselves to be swept along by it.

God's people are called to stand out from the culture in our sexual behaviour, rather than allow ourselves to be swept along by it.

We see the same instruction in New Testament times. Corinth, for example, was renowned as a city where anything went sexually. The city's reputation was so bad that to 'corinthianize' meant to live a sexually promiscuous life. And in writing to the church at Corinth, Paul urges believers to have a different sexual ethic, to 'flee from sexual immorality' (1 Corinthians 6:18).

Now, some people reject Paul's views on sexuality, claiming to like the teachings of Jesus better. Paul is accused unfairly of being homophobic and anti-women. But Jesus won't allow this, as he is speaking authoritatively through his personally commissioned apostle (meaning 'sent one' or 'envoy'). So if we reject Paul, we are rejecting Jesus.

But isn't it a question of justice?

In 2,000 years little has changed. We face exactly the same kind of challenges today. In terms of sexual ethics, Corinth is really not all that different from every major city in the world. Pretty much anything goes sexually, and everyone decides for themselves what is morally acceptable. Increasingly, of course, morals don't even come into it. No, we speak the language of rights.

Annabel, an undergraduate student, put it like this when I spoke at an evangelistic event organized by Cambridge University Christian Union: 'I think people should have a right to choose how to live sexually, and I'm not prepared to believe in a God who would deny people that fundamental human right.'

But followers of Jesus Christ, the one who gave up his rights for our sake, are called to think and behave differently. The Christian life is a counter-cultural life. In fact, Jesus says we're 'the salt of the earth' (a preservative stemming moral decay) and 'the light of the world' (shining into moral darkness). So if we adopt the same sexual ethic as our culture, or have no sexual ethics at all, then we both dishonour Jesus and damage our witness to a lost and confused world.

But doesn't Jesus want us to be happy?

Diver and Olympic bronze medallist Tom Daley posted a video on YouTube in which he claimed,

I met someone and they make me feel so happy, so safe, and everything feels just great, and that someone is a guy . . . of course, I still fancy girls, but I mean, right now I'm dating a guy and I couldn't be happier.[5]

His fans and the media alike generally received Tom's coming out statement very positively, reflecting the cultural shift over the last couple of generations. We now measure the legitimacy of our relationships according to whether or not they bring us personal happiness.

Rob spoke at one church about his decision to be celibate out of love for, and obedience to, Jesus Christ. And someone, not a Christian, asked him, 'But doesn't Jesus want you to be happy?'

It's an interesting question. For the Christian, the answer depends on what is meant by the word 'happy'. Paul commands Christians in Philippi to 'rejoice in the Lord always', and then repeats himself – presumably to avoid all doubt – 'I will say it again: rejoice!' (Philippians 4:4). And the apostle Peter writes of 'an inexpressible and glorious joy' that comes to us through a knowledge of, and love for, Jesus Christ (1 Peter 1:8).

So we're not to be motivated by the pursuit of superficial, temporary happiness which is always fluctuating according to our state of mind, feelings or circumstances. God has something much, much better for us. He offers deep and lasting joy that's inexpressible and rooted in a loving relationship with Jesus Christ. The Jesus who says to his followers, 'If you love me, keep my commands' (John 14:15).

Painful but promising

As we've seen, Jesus clearly teaches that same-sex practice is sinful. And there's no denying that this is a tough truth. Tough for us both, and for many of you reading this book too, or for friends whom you know, or for a family member, or someone in your church. The reality is, though, that the Law and the Prophets, the apostles and Jesus Christ himself are all consistent and clear. They all agree that the only God-given environment for love and attraction to express themselves sexually is within heterosexual marriage.

So where does this leave the same-sex attracted Christian longing for intimacy and companionship who doesn't want to live life alone? We'll come to the question of intimacy in chapters 10 and 11. Surely the place to start, though, is by focusing on the Lord Jesus and his sufficiency. If we're to stick to the narrow road that leads to abundant life, then we need to be fully convinced that Jesus is enough, that he's willing and able to provide for all our needs.

5. EVERYTHING YOU NEED?

I am the bread of life. Whoever comes to me will never go hungry, and whoever believes in me will never be thirsty.
(John 6:35)

Is your God too small? Rob's story

'That's Orion's Belt,' said Dad, as Charlie pulled sharply on the lead, eager to press on with the walk. We regularly took the dog out together. On a clear night Dad enjoyed pointing out various stars and constellations to me. As a teenager, the sheer scale of God's creation overwhelmed and fascinated me. I was in awe of Almighty God who had flung the stars into space. I believed that a God with such immeasurable power could do anything, and was convinced he could provide for all my needs. True, he didn't answer my prayer to be able to walk on water at the local lake. But I had to concede that I didn't actually *need* to do that.

As I grew up out of my childlike faith, sadly, my God seemed to shrink. Sex was everywhere: friends were talking about it, advertisers were shamelessly using it to sell products, and I was facing a constant barrage of images that were making it seemingly impossible to avoid. I had always believed that God created the good gift of sex to be enjoyed exclusively within heterosexual marriage, but I was being fed a lie that I needed to have sex to be happy. In a culture where sex had become a god, was the one true God powerful enough to provide for me if I pursued a life of celibacy? Was it possible to be satisfied in Christ without a sexual relationship?

On those occasions when I gave in to sexual temptation and entered a brief relationship, I evidently didn't believe that God was powerful enough to provide for me, and wasn't convinced that the love of Christ was sufficient to satisfy my deepest longings and that he was the source of genuine delight. I gave in to that ancient temptation and believed the lie that the Lord was withholding from me something good, pleasing and desirable.

'We shall never want to serve God in our real and secret hearts if he looms in our subconscious mind as an arbitrary Dictator or a Spoil-sport,' wrote Bible scholar J. B. Phillips, 'or as one who takes advantage of his position to make us poor mortals feel guilty and afraid. We have not only to be impressed by the "size" and unlimited power of God, we have to be moved to genuine admiration, respect, and affection, if we are ever to worship him.'[1]

Is your God too small? The Bible asserts that everything I need to live a satisfying, God-honouring life is found in and through a relationship with Christ: 'His divine power has given us everything we need for a godly life through our knowledge of him who called us by his own glory and good-ness' (2 Peter 1:3).

So the Lord Jesus deserves my genuine admiration, respect and affection. More than anyone or anything else. Increasingly, I need to delight in him and find my ultimate satisfaction in him. He really is sufficient.

Sufficient because he is supreme

No-one is greater or more powerful than Jesus Christ. If we doubt this truth, then we'll struggle to believe that Christ is sufficient. His sufficiency flows from his supremacy. The existence of a greater, more powerful being would mean that Christ lacks something, that he is deficient in some way. But he lacks nothing: 'For God was pleased to have all his fullness dwell in him' (Colossians 1:19), and he is 'the Messiah, who is God over all' (Romans 9:5).

Jesus, the Lord in creation

Everything was created through and for Jesus Christ. Everything. 'For in him all things were created: things in heaven and on earth, visible and invisible, whether thrones or powers or rulers or authorities; all things have been created through him and for him' (Colossians 1:16). The apostle John also unveils Jesus, the Word, as the Creator of all things:

> In the beginning was the Word, and the Word was with God, and the Word was God. He was with God in the beginning. Through him all things were made; without him nothing was made that has been made. In him was life, and that life was the light of all mankind.
> (John 1:1–4)

If everything has been made 'through him and for him', then this means that you and I were also created through and for Jesus Christ. He made you for his own glory, and brought you into this world. You are not your own. And the one who has power and authority to create life itself is also sufficient and able to provide everything you need to live a life that glorifies him. There is nothing we need for a satisfied life that can be found outside of a relationship with Jesus Christ.

Jesus, the amazing Sustainer

The diameter of the 'observable' universe spans 93 billion light years, scientists estimate, and contains around 170 billion galaxies.[2] Just think, Jesus holds it all together by his supreme power: 'He is before all things, and in him all things hold together' (Colossians 1:17). Elsewhere God urges us to take a look at at the sky for evidence of his incomparable power:

> 'To whom will you compare me?
>   Or who is my equal?' says the Holy One.
> Lift up your eyes and look to the heavens:
>   who created all these?
> He who brings out the starry host one by one
>   and calls forth each of them by name.
> Because of his great power and mighty strength,
>   not one of them is missing.
> (Isaiah 40:25–26)

But can someone who controls the whole universe really be concerned with the nuts and bolts of planet Earth too? Absolutely. He ensures that we're precisely the right distance from the sun: too near and the water essential for life would evaporate, too far away and our planet would be too cold for life. Earth must also rotate at the correct speed: too slow and we would face extreme differences in temperature between day and night, too fast and wind speeds would be catastrophic.

Fair enough. But with all that big-picture thinking to do, is Jesus really able to pay meticulous attention to the finer details? The minutiae of my body, for example?

Yes! At the other end of the scale from galaxies, solar systems and planets, Jesus also exercises sovereign control over the intricacies of the human body. The average human brain has approximately 86 billion neurones.[3] If uncoiled, the DNA in all the cells of your body would stretch around 10 billion miles, which is the equivalent of to Pluto and back again![4]

Jesus is the divine maestro, with planetary positions, brain-power and our DNA all perfectly orchestrated by him. The one who has the power to hold everything in the universe together can also be trusted with every detail of our lives. Even the very hairs of our heads – not too many, in my, Jonathan's, case – are numbered (Luke 12:7).

Amazingly, Jesus doesn't sustain us remotely, from a distance. No, his name is Immanuel (God with us). As an unmarried man, with no human partner to help me through difficult times, I find it so encouraging to remind myself that the Creator and Sustainer of all things dwells within me by the Holy Spirit. This is really worth pondering. If you're a Christian, the all-powerful, sovereign Maker of everything has taken up residence in you by his Spirit. Permanently. Jesus promises his disciples in John 14:16 that this advocate will 'help you and be with you *for ever*' (italics mine).

Jesus, the head of the body

Jesus 'is the head of the body, the church; he is the beginning and the firstborn from among the dead, so that in everything he might have the supremacy' (Colossians 1:18). The body of Christ, the church, is immense and ever-expanding. We're not talking here about denominations, or buildings, or institution-alized religion, but the 'invisible' church: all those who are trusting in Jesus Christ as Lord and Saviour. This consists of an eclectic mix of countless believers from all times, of all ages, from all nations and diverse cultural, social, religious and racial backgrounds. Jesus, the first to be resurrected from the dead, is the supreme head of this vast body.

As a young Christian, I (Jonathan) sometimes struggled to feel at home in my local church. Not because people weren't welcoming or loving: I was fortunate to be surrounded by Christian brothers and sisters who genuinely cared for me. The problem was that most didn't know about my background or my ongoing same-sex temptations. Homosexuality was much more of a taboo issue in the 1990s than it is today.

I felt lonely and craved intimacy. There were times when I longed to be more open and honest about my same-sex attractions, not least to try to deter those well-meaning Christians who loved to play Cupid by attempting to find me a girlfriend! My persistent fear of being rejected by this new community meant that, sadly, I generally kept my struggle hidden.

How I wish I'd had the courage in those early days to share this battle with more Christians in my circle. Occasionally on a Friday or Saturday night I would end up in a gay bar. I wasn't looking for a sexual encounter but, rather, just seeking a sense of belonging and acceptance. In that environment I felt I could be myself, with no need to hide the fact that I was attracted to people of the same sex. The Lord Jesus challenged this way of thinking, and convinced me, over time, that I needed to pursue this sense of belonging and acceptance within the body of Christ.

Accepting one another, just as Christ has accepted us, is an essential element of Christian community, and a church glorifies God when it does this (Romans 15:7). I slowly realized that, by going to gay bars, I'd been looking for acceptance outside of Christ's body, as if he were somehow insufficient. I needed to trust that, as the head of the body, Jesus was powerful enough to provide me with Christian brothers and sisters who would accept me in Christ, with all my weaknesses and ongoing struggles.

So how can a local church help to support Christians struggling with same-sex attractions? They can do this by creating a loving, accepting community where people feel able to be open about their struggles. And by looking out for those who might be feeling marginalized or alienated.

Sufficient to satisfy our desires?

I love the encounter between Jesus and the unnamed woman of Samaria, recorded in John's Gospel. He meets her at Jacob's well and declares that he's able to give her living water. She questions his ability to draw water from the well, but Jesus has a very different kind of refreshment in mind:

> Everyone who drinks this water will be thirsty again, but whoever drinks the water I give them will never thirst. Indeed, the water I give them will become in them a spring of water welling up to eternal life.
> (John 4:13–14)

She asks him to give her some of this water. But Jesus tells her to go, call her husband and come back. It then becomes clear that this woman has been married five times and is now living with a man she's not married to. Now, why does Jesus appear to change the subject so abruptly? He has just offered living water that provides eternal satisfaction, but then suddenly he exposes her messed-up sex life. Why? What's the connection?

We don't know if her previous marriages ended through bereavement or divorce, or a combination of the two. But the implication seems to be that for years she's been pursuing satisfaction and fulfilment in relationships, trying to satisfy her deepest longings in the arms of men. And looking to sex and lust, or to physical intimacy, or emotional connection, for the kind of deep comfort, love and affirmation that only Jesus can give hasn't worked. It never does. Before I was a Christian, I used to characterize God in my mind as a kind of cosmic killjoy. I just didn't get why he was opposed to gay relationships, and imagined him looking down from heaven devising schemes to deny his creatures pleasure.

> *The God who creates us with desires also delights to satisfy those desires.*

I could not have been more wrong. As we saw earlier, this is what Satan wants us to believe. But human desire is inbuilt by God, and the God who creates us with desires also delights to satisfy those desires. But satisfy them with good things, ultimately, with the living water that is Christ.

I heard the voice of Jesus say,
'Behold, I freely give
the living water; thirsty one;
stoop down and drink, and live.'[5]

We will miss out on those good things if we pursue a same-sex relationship or seek satisfaction through illicit sexual encounters. I must believe that God, the one who determines what is good and what is evil, has something better for me. And if I deny myself a same-sex relationship out of love for, and obedience to, Jesus Christ, I'm not denying myself something good, pleasing and desirable at all. If I drink water from his well, by contrast, he promises that I will never thirst. Indeed, this water will well up inside me to eternal life.

The psalmist suggests that if the Lord satisfies my desires with good things, then I may even feel young again. (Now wouldn't that be nice?)

> Praise the LORD, my soul;
>> all my inmost being, praise his holy name.
> Praise the LORD, my soul,
>> and forget not all his benefits –
> who forgives all your sins
>> and heals all your diseases,
> who redeems your life from the pit
>> and crowns you with love and compassion,
> who satisfies your desires with good things
>> so that your youth is renewed like the eagle's.
> (Psalm 103:1–5)

So will I seek satisfaction in and through a relationship with Christ, or will I try to fulfil my desires apart from him? Will I trust the all-wise Creator and Sustainer of the universe to satisfy me with good things? To do so is to believe that, as the seventeenth-century pastor and author John Flavel puts it,

> Christ is the very essence of all delights and pleasures, the very soul and substance of them. As all the rivers are gathered into the ocean, which is the meeting-place of all the waters in the world, so Christ is that ocean in which all true delights and pleasures meet.[6]

Sufficient to strengthen us in temptation?

Oscar Wilde's fictional character Lord Henry Wotton suggested that 'the only way to get rid of a temptation is to yield to it'.[7] As Christians, we must think differently. We need to believe, first, that greater pleasure is found in resisting temptation and delighting to do our Father's will. Jesus is our model here, the pioneer and perfecter of our faith, who 'for the joy that was set before him . . . endured the cross' (Hebrews 12:2).

We need to believe, secondly, that Christ is sufficient to strengthen us when we face temptation. Paul prays for the Ephesians, that God 'may strengthen you with power through his Spirit in your inner being, so that Christ may dwell in your hearts through faith' (Ephesians 3:16–17). We can definitely trust in the sufficiency of the indwelling Spirit of Christ to strengthen us in temptation, because of:

The unique nature of Jesus
Fully God

The child to be born as God's Messiah, according to Isaiah's prophecy, 'will be called Wonderful Counsellor, Mighty God, Everlasting Father, Prince of Peace' (Isaiah 9:6). The miraculous works of Jesus in the Gospels display the truth that he is this long-promised Divine Rescuer, in whom all the fullness of God dwells. He only has to say the word, and the demons flee, the storm is calmed, the blind see, the dead are raised. Jesus is omnipotent (all-powerful): all authority in heaven and on earth has been given to him (Matthew 28:18). So he has complete power over all our temptations.

One of the keys to resisting temptation is to hold on to the truth that Jesus is God, infinitely more powerful than the strongest of sinful desires in our hearts and the fiercest of fiery arrows that the tempter can hurl at us. When temptation rages, we should feel confident because, whatever forces are ranged against us, Jesus is for us. He has the power to protect us in, and deliver us from, temptation:

To him who is able to keep you from stumbling and to present you before his glorious presence without fault and with great joy – to the only God our Saviour be glory, majesty, power and authority, through Jesus Christ our Lord, before all ages, now and for evermore! Amen.

(Jude 24–25)

Fully man

He slept. He ate. He drank. He wept. He was severely tempted. When he stepped into this world, remarkably, the Mighty God of Isaiah 9:6 shared in our humanity. Jesus had to be made like us: 'fully human in every way, in order that he might become a merciful and faithful high priest in service to God, and that he might make atonement for the sins of the people. Because he suffered when he was tempted, he is able to help those who are being tempted' (Hebrews 2:17–18).

Take me home now

As a young Christian, I would sometimes stretch out on my sofa and, exasperated, tearfully pour out my heart to God. I'd plead with him in those anguished moments to let me go to heaven *now*. Still today I can get weary of always fighting, resisting and saying no. And in the heat of the battle resisting same-sex temptations, I get frustrated at times with God. Or doubt that he understands how difficult it is to stand firm. In fact, I've often asked myself, 'Does God really "get" it?'

Jesus' temptations were genuine. He confronted and resisted them as a man, but never once gave in to them. 'A man who gives in to temptation after five minutes,' writes C. S. Lewis, 'simply does not know what it would have been like an hour later . . . We never find out the strength of the evil impulse inside us until we try to fight it: and Christ, because he was the only man who never yielded to temptation, is also the only man who knows to the full what temptation means – the only complete realist.'[8]

Christ suffered when he was tempted more than I can possibly comprehend. He was beaten, mocked, insulted, stripped, humiliated, crucified alongside common criminals. Worst of all, he bore the wrath of God and was separated from the perfect heavenly communion he enjoyed with his Father: 'My God, my God, why have you forsaken me?' (Matthew 27:46).

So we can say with confidence, Jesus definitely 'gets it'. The loneliness, the fear, the doubt, the anguish, the frustration, the longing for heaven. Not only that, but he really is able to help those who are being tempted:

> For we do not have a high priest who is unable to feel sympathy for our weaknesses, but we have one who has been tempted in every way, just as we are – yet he did not sin. Let us then approach God's throne of grace with confidence, so that we may receive mercy and find grace to help us in our time of need. (Hebrews 4:15–16)

Sufficient to deal with our failure?

If you were accused of a crime, wouldn't you want to employ the finest legal representation available?

Our adversary, Satan, accuses us of crimes before God day and night (Revelation 12:10). But, thankfully, we have the ultimate Defence Lawyer representing us before the Holy One: 'an advocate with the Father – Jesus Christ, the Righteous One. He is the atoning sacrifice for our sins, and not only for ours but also for the sins of the whole world' (1 John 2:1).

This side of heaven there will be times when we fail to draw on Christ's strength to resist temptation and we fall into sin.

Satan loves to accuse us on those occasions, particularly if we consider ourselves guilty of serious moral failure. But Christ is our advocate. He pleads with the Father on our behalf.

What is our defence though? We failed to resist, and we fell into sin – surely it is case closed, guilty as charged? We may argue that there are mitigating circumstances, but ultimately we're without excuse, for 'when you are tempted, he will also provide a way out so that you can endure it' (1 Corinthians 10:13).

Here is our only defence: justice has already been dispensed; Jesus has already been punished in my place; he has paid for my crimes. It is indeed case closed.

> When Satan tempts me to despair
> And tells me of the guilt within,
> Upward I look and see Him there
> Who made an end of all my sin.
> Because the sinless Saviour died
> My sinful soul is counted free.
> For God the just is satisfied
> To look on Him and pardon me.[9]

But what if I fall over and over again, and find myself trapped in a cycle of ungodly behaviour? As we saw earlier, there have been times in my Christian life when I have been enslaved to pornography, and have had to be led back to repentance.

Is Jesus really sufficient to deal with that kind of repeated failure? What hope is there for a persistent offender?

6. GRIPPED BY GRACE

For the grace of God has appeared that offers salvation
to all people. It teaches us to say 'No' to ungodliness
and worldly passions, and to live self-controlled,
upright and godly lives in this present age.
(Titus 2:11–12)

Back to Egypt?

I carefully arranged the roast potatoes, carrots and runner beans around the slightly charred chicken pie and ladled a liberal helping of rich gravy over everything, just as he liked it. Archie was my favourite. He usually had a funny story to share. The more I laughed, the less I seemed to notice his missing front teeth and the unfortunate aroma of a week of sleeping rough.

I'd been a Christian for around three years now. Helping out at the local homeless outreach was one of the many activities into which I threw myself with high energy and enthusiasm. Serving others and keeping busy was a major part of my coping strategy, partially dulling the pain of what I was missing most: intimacy.

Ben (in chapter 3) and I were still close. And that despite my emotional intensity and occasional jealous outburst. He always kept calm. God gave him the grace to put up with way more than any friend should ever have had to. He saw it, I think, as his personal mission to stick with me in Christlike love. And to encourage me as I learned (ever so slowly) how to develop godly, non-erotic love for a Christian brother. Ben was a great friend. But he was also a straight friend. Somehow his friendship, no matter how close and unconditional, just wasn't enough. I wanted more. I wanted something, or someone, to dull the pain of the loneliness.

I'd been praying and pleading with God to change my sexual attractions. I longed to get married and be a father. But nothing had changed. Despite some counselling, I was no more attracted to women than when I had first come to faith. And more importantly, I was still attracted to men. Why wasn't God answering?

In the midst of this frustration and hunger for intimacy, I met Jack. Well, I 'met' him online. The internet was new and pretty basic back then. And slow. Very slow. But even in its mostly innocent infancy it opened up a whole new world to me, a way to connect with others from different parts of the country and around the world. Online chat would satisfy (or so I thought) my craving for intimacy and connection. But it quickly became a snare to me.

When I finally found the courage to meet Jack some months later, the plan was just to talk face to face. He was looking for an 'affectionate friendship' rather than a relationship, and seemed to fully respect my Christian faith. 'So what's the worst that could happen?', I thought to myself. I smiled as I recalled one of the famous Dr Pepper TV adverts. Deep down I think I always knew I was deceiving myself. So it was hardly surprising when, from a faith perspective, the worst that could happen did happen. Our affectionate friendship turned sexual.

I carried on going to church. I carried on feeding homeless people and helping out at a coffee bar for international students and co-leading a home group and preaching on the street and singing in the music group. But now my relentless Christian service was an attempt not to paper over the cracks of a lonely life, but to conceal the guilt of a hidden life. After only three years of following Jesus, I was making the same mistake as the Israelites in the Old Testament, and looking back – even turning back – to Egypt. Back to my slavery to sin, from which God had so graciously rescued me.

Don't be deceived

We've seen already that the serpent's lie in the Garden of Eden helped give birth to humankind's rebellion against God. As a result, we all need to guard against both the devil's deception and the deceitfulness of our own hearts. Paul warns the Corinthian Christians about the danger of being deceived on matters of salvation:

> Or do you not know that wrongdoers will not inherit the kingdom of God? Do not be deceived: neither the sexually immoral nor idolaters nor adulterers nor men who have sex with men nor thieves nor the greedy nor drunkards nor slanderers nor swindlers will inherit the kingdom of God.
> (1 Corinthians 6:9–10)

Try to imagine Christians in that Corinthian church circa AD 55 as Paul's letter is being read out. Think of the impact his stark words would have had. The implication is that they cannot with any integrity call themselves Christians and continue to live in the various ways outlined with no evidence of repentance. So they cannot go on committing adultery, getting drunk, stealing, slandering or defrauding people. This cannot be the ongoing pattern of their lives. Paul is not writing about matters of behaviour over which the Corinthians can just 'agree to disagree' with the apostle. No, these are all marks of unrighteousness, characteristics of people not inheriting the kingdom of God.

Included in this list, of course, are 'men who have sex with men'. Now this is a paraphrase of two Greek words: *malakoi* and *arsenokoitai*. *Malakoi* means the 'soft ones' or 'effeminate ones'. The term *arsenokoitai* is a compound Greek word, with its roots in the Greek translation of the Old Testament, the Scriptures Paul would have used, known as the Septuagint. In that translation both Leviticus 18:22 and Leviticus 20:13 prohibit a man (*arsenos*) from lying sexually with (*koitēn*) another man. By using both *malakoi* and *arsenokoitai*, Paul is clear and unambiguous. He states that any form of same-sex practice is a mark of unrighteousness.

What some of you were

But what about those in the Corinthian church who had come to faith from a background of same-sex practice? Some of them used to live in the various ways outlined. So if they were still struggling with same-sex desires or had perhaps recently given in to sexual temptation, does this mean they were now excluded from the kingdom of God? This is a critical question, because it has serious implications for those reading (and writing) this book who have fallen or failed sexually as Christians.

This is why we need to let scripture interpret scripture. Now we know from Paul's other writings that our salvation is not a reward for good behaviour. How many of us were told when we were little, 'Now be good, or Santa won't bring you any presents'? This sort of statement reinforces the idea that bad people get punished and good people get rewarded.

But the gospel obliterates that way of thinking. God is not in the business of giving the gift of eternal life to decent, moral people. And heaven is not a reward for well-behaved children – it's an utterly undeserved gift of grace. And, paradoxically, it is given only to those who recognize that their own righteousness will never be enough to earn a place in God's kingdom: 'For it is by grace you have been saved, through faith – and this is not from yourselves, it is the gift of God – not by works, so that no one can boast' (Ephesians 2:8–9).

So we can be sure that Paul does not intend the Corinthians to believe that *because* they turn away from his list of vices, *therefore* they inherit the kingdom of God. No, that would be salvation by works. The gospel of grace is completely counter-intuitive. *Because* the Corinthians have inherited the kingdom of God by grace alone, *therefore* they must turn away from ungodly behaviour. Their ongoing repentance is evidence of the genuineness of their faith.

So, having warned these Christians in Corinth not to be deceived, Paul then goes on to reassure them of their secure position in Christ: 'And that is what some of you were. But you were washed, you were sanctified, you were justified, in the name of the Lord Jesus Christ and by the Spirit of our God' (1 Corinthians 6:11).

The NET Bible translates 'That is what some of you were' as 'Some of you once lived this way.' So there were Christians in the Corinthian church who had once lived in the various ways outlined in 1 Corinthians 6:9–10. Some had been involved in same-sex practice. The implication, of course, is that they don't live that way any more. Why? Clearly, they've had a saving, life-changing encounter with Jesus Christ; they have believed and responded to the gospel.

Actually, all of us once lived in the kinds of ways Paul outlines in the above passage. As he writes elsewhere, 'There is no one righteous, not even one' (Romans 3:10). It's important always to remember that the church is made up not of good people, but of rescued sinners. An authentic gospel church will be full of people who used to live in a whole variety of sinful ways, but who are now being transformed by the Holy Spirit to live in new and godly ways.

If you struggle with same-sex temptations, then remember, we're no longer identified as those who have sex with people of the same sex. That's not who we are, or what we do, any more. As we'll see in the next chapter, we now have a new identity, and now bear the name of Jesus Christ.

It's important always to remember that the church is made up not of good people, but of rescued sinners.

One of the major pieces of evidence that our faith is genuine is that, increasingly, we turn away from all kinds of unrighteous behaviour. Yes, we're saved by grace through faith in Jesus Christ. But we mustn't be deceived into thinking we can call ourselves citizens of heaven and carry on living however we like, without tangible signs of repentance. Paul reminds us of three vital truths, a trio of glorious aspects to our redemption, or rescue, that will both challenge and reassure us.

Three vital truths

You were washed
It really doesn't matter who you are, or where you've been, or what you've done. If you're trusting in Jesus' death on the

cross, then your sins have been washed away by the blood of the Lamb. The slate is wiped completely clean. This is symbolized in and through baptism. So after his conversion Paul was told: 'Get up, be baptised and wash your sins away, calling on his name' (Acts 22:16).

Many same-sex attracted Christians find it really difficult to believe this glorious truth or apply it to themselves. They are burdened with the guilt and shame of past failures or ongoing weaknesses, and this inhibits the joy of their salvation. If this is true of you (or someone you're supporting), then the most effective remedy I know is prayerfully to immerse yourself in Scripture. And in particular those passages that speak of the incredible sacrifice of Jesus Christ in your place and on your behalf (Isaiah 53, for example, or Romans 5:6–11).

Or remind yourself perhaps that 'as far as the east is from the west, so far has he removed our transgressions from us' (Psalm 103:12). How far exactly is the east from the west? Well, it depends on what we measure, and at which point we fix east and west. So east to west around the circumference of the earth would be around 24,874 miles.[1] That's a pretty long way. I'd be quite content knowing that God had removed my sins and placed them nearly 25,000 miles away. But the reality is infinitely better. God deliberately chooses to remember them no more.

If you struggle to believe the reality that God has removed your sins, then keep asking him to make real to you the truth of being washed 'in the name of the Lord Jesus Christ and by the Spirit of our God' (1 Corinthians 6:11). Or why not ask someone, a friend or a Christian leader perhaps, to read Scripture with you and to pray for, or with, you? Sometimes it can be so helpful to hear someone speaking out biblical truths about God's forgiveness. As they do so, the Holy Spirit can minister this reality to your heart.

I did this with a young man, Oliver, who just could not accept that God had forgiven him. He'd been in a same-sex relationship for a brief period while also serving as a youth worker. We met for a few weeks, and I read Scripture to him and prayed for him, asking the Holy Spirit to help him accept God's forgiveness in his heart. I knew these prayers had been answered when one week he finally prayed aloud himself, with tears, thanking God for his amazing grace and forgiveness. From that point on Oliver was different. I could see in his face that he'd been released from the burden of guilt and was now experiencing the joy of God's salvation.

> He breaks the power of cancelled sin,
> he sets the prisoner free;
> his blood can make the foulest clean;
> his blood availed for me.[2]

You were sanctified

Being sanctified (made holy) has something of a bad press. I'm sure most of us can think of people who come across as sanctimonious or 'holier than thou', those who feel morally superior. This kind of behaviour gives Christians a bad name. I know a number of gay and lesbian people who've been harshly judged and looked down upon by modern-day Pharisees. But remember that haughty eyes are one of 'six things that the LORD hates, seven that are an abomination to him' (Proverbs 6:16–17 ESV). Those who are truly sanctified, in contrast, will be marked out by grace and humility as they reflect the beautiful holiness of Jesus Christ. To be holy is to be like Jesus.

Sanctification is past, present and future. When we first trusted in Jesus, we *were* sanctified, that is, set apart from sin to God, and made holy and precious in his sight. This was an act of pure grace. If this leads to us looking down on others in moral superiority, then we've completely missed the point.

We're also *being* sanctified, conformed to the likeness of Jesus in our attitudes and behaviour. Becoming practically what God has already declared us to be as a spiritual reality. The Holy Spirit is the agent of our sanctification, driving home God's truth to our hearts and transforming us from the inside out. Jesus prays for his disciples, 'Sanctify them by the truth; your word is truth' (John 17:17). The Spirit of God works in union with the word of God to make us holy. Therefore the more seriously we take God's word in the Bible, the more we'll aid the process of sanctification in our lives.

Now this work of transformation is an ongoing process, and patience is needed. As you know, I have pastorally supported people who've come to faith either from a promiscuous background or out of a long-term same-sex partnership. And it often takes time to turn away from past habits and actions.

That's not to say, of course, that the Holy Spirit might not sometimes intervene in quite striking ways. This happened with a friend of mine called Debbie. Her civil partner left her after a five-year relationship. To use her own words, she 'went wild' and slept around for just over a year. A work colleague then shared the gospel with her, and she began to attend an Alpha course. She came to faith three months later and within days had turned away from all same-sex practice. Within weeks her same-sex desires had all but vanished. Five years on and she's now married to Anthony and they have two children. Apart from the occasional unhelpful dream, Debbie tells me she no longer experiences any same-sex temptations.

This kind of dramatic turnaround story is rare. Generally, it takes time for the word of God and the Spirit of God to bring about the necessary deep conviction that leads to tangible changes in behaviour. So I sometimes have to gently manage the expectations of same-sex attracted Christians and those seeking to support them.

Finally, we *will be* sanctified. On that last day when Christ appears to wrap up this world and usher in the new heavens and earth, 'we shall be like him, for we shall see him as he is' (1 John 3:2). Jesus is perfectly holy, and the ultimate goal of our sanctification is to become like him. You could not imagine anybody less sanctimonious or 'holier than thou' than the Lord Jesus.

You were justified

John travelled to Africa's west coast. He paid for his cargo as normal, then sailed off to the Caribbean. His cargo was people, and their conditions were horrific, for the year was 1750. The number who would have died on John's business trips is unknown. But what we do know is that this same man later went on to denounce the slave trade as a result of his faith in Jesus Christ. But after years as a people trafficker, could he ever be confident of his standing before God? John Newton wrote the now-famous words which suggest he had every confidence that he was now in the right with his Maker:

> Amazing grace! How sweet the sound
> That sav'd a wretch like me!
> I once was lost, but now am found,
> Was blind, but now I see.[3]

'Justified' is one of my favourite Christian terms: it means to be brought into a right relationship with God. The word has legal connotations. God has acquitted the justified person, declared them not guilty. He does not just write off my sins like an irrecoverable bad debt. Rather, he acquits me on the basis that Jesus has already paid the price. I'm guilty. I deserve God's wrath. But God is just and will never demand repayment of a debt that's already been fully satisfied by Christ on the cross. To be justified is to stand before God in his supreme court of justice and be treated as if I'd never sinned. As if I'd lived the perfect life that only Jesus lived, 'just-as-if-ied never sinned', as my Sunday school teacher used to say.

If you come from a background of same-sex practice, or struggle with same-sex temptations but are trusting in Jesus Christ, you can be full of confidence. Not proud self-confidence of course, but confidence rooted in the truth that in Christ you are 'in the right' with God.

You may often find yourself tormented by ungodly desires and longings that cause you to wonder if you really are a Christian at all. You may have lived a godless, chequered past and feel anxious about whether your very worst sins are indeed forgiven.

But Dr Martyn Lloyd-Jones reminds us that

> The very essence of the Christian faith is to say that he [Jesus] is good enough and I am in him . . . It doesn't matter if you have almost entered into the depths of hell. It does not matter if you are guilty of murder as well as every other vile sin. It does not matter from the standpoint of being justified before God at all. You are no more hopeless than the most moral and respectable person in the world.[4]

For those of us who wage an ongoing war against same-sex temptations, we can rest assured that 'since we have been justified through faith, we have peace with God through our Lord Jesus Christ' (Romans 5:1). If we're in Christ, then it's important not to beat ourselves up over past failures. To punish yourself is not to trust in the one who has already taken God's punishment on your behalf and in whose name you are now justified.

Remember,

> He was pierced for our transgressions,
>> he was crushed for our iniquities;
> the punishment that brought us peace was on him,
>> and by his wounds we are healed.

(Isaiah 53:5)

But what if I'm still experiencing same-sex attraction?

God quickly convicted me about the ungodly friendship with Jack and graciously led me to repentance. I recognized that I couldn't claim to be a Christian while continuing to engage in same-sex practice. God forgave my sin and reminded me that I was washed, sanctified and justified in the name of the Lord Jesus Christ.

Yet I continued to struggle. And some believers are quite surprised when I say this. At one church Raphael, a married man, quoted 1 Corinthians 6:11 and made the point that Paul writes, 'that is what some of you *were*', interpreting this to mean that some of the Corinthian Christians were gay, but that they're not gay any more. God had completely set them free from same-sex attractions and made them 'straight'.

But this is why I think the translation: 'some of you once lived this way' is more helpful. Paul is talking here about actions rather than attractions, or sins rather than temptations. This is a really important distinction. The Bible does not promise us that we'll be completely temptation-free in this life – quite the opposite in fact!

We need to grasp this distinction to effectively support those who struggle. Many are loaded with huge burdens of guilt already for simply finding people of the same sex attractive. But does the Bible really teach that finding someone attractive is, in and of itself, sinful? If so, then married Raphael is in trouble too. Because he admitted to me that he sometimes finds women other than his wife attractive.

Nowhere does the Bible teach that merely finding people attractive is sinful. Yes, of course, attraction can so easily lead to lust, which Jesus says is to commit adultery in our hearts (Matthew 5:28). So Raphael needs to decide what to do when he finds another woman attractive. Does he give in to the temptation to lust over her? Or does he metaphorically pluck out his eye so that he doesn't take that risky second glance (Matthew 5:29)?

I face that exact same dilemma when I see an attractive man. In one sense my temptations are really no different from Raphael's. And I have no need to feel guilty as long as I resist them.

'So you're still gay then?' Raphael asked.

'No, that's not who I am any more,' I replied.

7. BLURRED VISION

*For you died, and your life is now
hidden with Christ in God.*
(Colossians 3:3)

Who am I?

Many Christians who experience same-sex attraction face a
crisis of identity. What do I call myself? Am I a celibate gay
Christian, or a same-sex attracted Christian, or a Christian
who struggles with same-sex temptations? Or, if I'm now
married to someone of the opposite sex, am I ex-gay or
post-gay? Or maybe I should simply call myself a Christian.

We're not the only people who struggle to describe
ourselves. Social media giant Facebook launched a facility in
2014 enabling users to select one of over fifty – yes, fifty! –
gender options, including gender non-conforming, pan-gender
and two-spirit person. User feedback suggested that the
choices were still too restrictive, so they later introduced a
'free-form' field.

'We recognise,' said Facebook, 'that some people face challenges sharing their true gender identity with others, and this

setting gives people the ability to express themselves in an authentic way.'[1]

Defining our identity can be complex and confusing. Is it rooted in gender, class, vocation, ethnicity, religion, sexual orientation or political allegiance? Or do we perhaps have multiple identities? One key finding of a UK government report was that 'rather than having a single identity, people have several overlapping identities, which shift in emphasis in different life stages and environments'.[2]

More important, I think, than the particular label I use to describe myself is what that label might be revealing about how I view my core identity.

Under pressure

'So . . . um . . . do you, um . . . think I might be gay?' asked thirteen-year-old Tom, following a talk I'd given in his church youth group. His friends had all left, but Tom held back under the pretext of helping the leaders to tidy up.

'Well, why don't you tell me,' I gently inquired, 'what makes you think you might be?'

'Well . . . um . . . my best friend Dan and I, we're like really close, we love chilling and just, like, get on so well. We're into the same music; we're both United supporters; we're in a band together and . . . um . . . I just kinda love Dan. There's no-one else like him; I'd trust him with my life.'

As Tom spoke affectionately about this boy he'd grown up with, stumbling over his words, I sensed he was describing an amazingly close friendship. I picked up no sexual or romantic undertones at all. But like many children and teenagers, Tom felt under pressure to make an early declaration of his sexual orientation, as if this were the key to defining himself. He felt no sexual attraction to Dan or to any other boys. But he thought he must be gay, simply because he loved, admired and cherished his best friend.

'A few of my mates at school think I'm gay,' he added before heading off. 'They say I spend way too much time with Dan, and keep joking that he's my boyfriend. It kinda worries me.'

I explained to Tom that the Bible never refers to people as 'gay', 'lesbian', 'bisexual', 'straight' and so on. Now I know some Christians who find these labels, or others, useful as a shorthand way of describing their sexual attractions. And Christians who experience same-sex attraction may consider this integral to who they are, something that can't be neatly compartmentalized. But if we allow our sexual attractions to define us, then we risk being victims of spiritual identity theft, robbed of the blessings of our true identity.

Something old, something new

'So what do you do?'

Since committing myself to a new local church, this has been the most frequent question as I've chatted with new people. It's been interesting – to say the least – to see how people react when they discover that I lead a ministry that supports Christians struggling with same-sex temptations. But what I do, in many people's minds, is an essential part of who I am as a person (and in my case it's partly true, I guess!). As is where I live, what qualifications I have, whether I'm single or married, if I have children, and so on. We use all sorts of categories and markers to define who we are.

But as we know, when we trust in Jesus Christ, everything changes. My core identity is now 'in Christ', and 'if anyone is in Christ, the new creation has come: the old has gone, the new is here!' (2 Corinthians 5:17). In Christ your life has begun again; you've been gifted a fresh start. We're not talking here about renovation and improvement, or about a programme like *Changing Rooms*. Rather, God brings demolition of the old, followed by a brand-new build.

Paul speaks of this in terms of life and death, to stress the radical nature of this new beginning. He reminds the Christians in Colosse that they died and were raised again (Colossians 3:1–4), something that is true for every believer. When I trust in Jesus Christ for the forgiveness of my sins, I become united to him and share with him in his death and resurrection. I am 'in Christ', so what happens to him also happens to me. He died, so I died (to my old way of thinking and living). He was raised, so I was raised (to a new way of thinking and living).

Included in this new way of thinking and living is an entirely different way of defining ourselves. Because 'here there is no Gentile or Jew, circumcised or uncircumcised, barbarian, Scythian, slave or free, but Christ is all, and is in all' (Colossians 3:11) – all the barriers and categories that previously divided people are smashed down in Christ. These identifying markers no longer have prime importance, and are to be firmly relegated below the fact that I'm now in him.

Similarly, being in Christ is infinitely more important than who we are sexually attracted to. So the old me, aged seventeen, identified myself as gay; it was an important aspect of my identity. But the new me no longer identifies as gay. The new me is a new creation in Christ. This essential truth now defines me.

But aren't you denying who you really are?

Brad, a gay friend of mine from California, believes that I'm denying who I really am by not calling myself gay and not acting on my sexual attractions. One time, only half-joking, he even called me a 'self-homophobe' (don't worry, I've been called much worse). Obviously, I disagree with him.

I've tried to explain to Brad that gay is not who I really am. No, 'who I am' is a follower of Jesus. Yes, I'm a follower of Jesus who happens to be exclusively same-sex attracted; I certainly don't deny that. But the essential me is rooted 'in Christ', not in my sexual attractions. And it's because of my love for Jesus and my desire to obey him that I willingly deny myself a same-sex relationship.

As Christians, we should steer away from defining ourselves according to our work, or our social status, or our sexual attractions, or any other factor that might be significant to us. Instead, we should build our identity around who we are and all that we have in Christ. Paul teaches Christians that God 'has blessed us in the heavenly realms with *every* spiritual blessing in Christ' (Ephesians 1:3, italics mine).

It's worth pausing and reflecting on that incredible fact for a moment. By implication, there is not a single spiritual blessing that can come to us outside of, or apart from, our relationship with Jesus Christ. Not even one. And these blessings are not far off and unreachable, but are earthed in practical reality. As we understand and grasp the immense privileges that are ours through being united with Christ, so our outlook on life can be radically transformed.

I can see clearly now

How then can we go about practically shaping our identity around who we are and what we have in Christ? Here are just a few examples of things that are true of us 'in Christ'. We have:

- eternal life (Romans 6:23)
- no condemnation (Romans 8:1)

- freedom (Galatians 2:4)
- the peace of God (Philippians 4:7).

We have many other spiritual blessings too. You might find it really encouraging to search them out, write them down, and prayerfully reflect on them. We saw in chapter 5 how God loves to satisfy our desires with good things. So why not ask God to help you see his spiritual blessings more clearly? And perhaps ask him increasingly to satisfy your heart with these wonderful realities.

If we identify ourselves according to who we really are – beneficiaries of every spiritual blessing in Christ – then we put ourselves in an excellent position to experience and enjoy the abundant life that Jesus promises. But if we construct our core identity around who we're sexually attracted to, or anything else that might be important to us, then we'll likely fail to see and experience the countless blessings that are ours. Remember, you died, and your life is now hidden with Christ in God (Colossians 3:3).

Narrow road, narrow vision

To give up a gay identity and deny oneself a same-sex relation-ship can be incredibly costly and difficult. From the perspective of this world alone, why would anyone do this? Why indeed? But from the viewpoint of eternity, the cost begins to make sense. Let's listen to Jesus in the Sermon on the Mount:

> Enter through the narrow gate. For wide is the gate and broad is the road that leads to destruction, and many enter through it. But small is the gate and narrow the road that leads to life, and only a few find it.
>
> (Matthew 7:13–14)

Do you notice the remarkable paradox here? Jesus urges us to enter through the narrow gate that leads to a narrow road. Narrow sounds like a very negative word. It might even make you think about narrow-minded people. And so you might assume that a narrow gate and a narrow road can only lead to an unsatisfying life of restriction. Surely, if we choose this way, our choice will suffocate us and lead us into a very limited and unfulfilling life?

But no. Here's the paradox. The narrow road, says Jesus, despite first appearances, 'leads to life'. So the apparently restrictive, suffocating road – an unpopular way which 'only a few find' – is actually the one that leads us out into a spacious place of abundant life and true freedom.

Let's be honest, it's certainly not popular today to speak about turning away from a gay identity or saying no to a same-sex relationship. We're assured, though, that whoever is prepared to lose his life for the sake of following Jesus will find it (Matthew 16:25). And we're now going to explore some ways in which same-sex attracted believers – and indeed any believer – can begin to enjoy this fullness of life. But it begins, just as Jesus says, by a willingness to lose it all.

PART 2:
LIVING THE ABUNDANT LIFE
ON THE NARROW ROAD

8. LIVING SACRIFICE

Do you not know that your bodies are temples of the
Holy Spirit . . . ? You are not your own; you were bought
at a price. Therefore honour God with your bodies.
(1 Corinthians 6:19–20)

Skin deep

Everywhere I turn, stunningly good-looking people are trying
to sell me something. Whether on TV, billboards, in magazines,
newspapers or online ads, it seems unavoidable.

I'm up early with a mission. I need a few clothes for an
upcoming holiday. I start online, and polo shirts are my first
Google search. Every model on every website looks perfect.
'Sure those colours look great on them,' I think to myself, 'but
can I honestly pull off bright pink?' My good friend Monica
would utter a short, sharp 'no way, Jonathan'.

In the shopping centre, I meet Cristiano Ronaldo, Justin
Bieber and David Beckham, each trying to flog me underwear,
so I walk in a zigzag pattern trying desperately to avoid the
unhelpful floor-to-ceiling adverts. I purchase my shirts and
head off to buy some jeans, pondering if it's really necessary
for the man in the poster to model the jeans with his top off.

At the end of a busy day of shopping I get home, put my feet up and switch on the TV. After dozing off and annoyingly missing the news, I wake up to find a scantily clad, bronzed and super-toned man running across my TV screen. What kind of programme is this? But he turns out to be advertising a cologne: 'Je suis sexy' or something similar.

Advertisers want to convince us that looks are not just skin-deep; they're vital. They set a standard which most of us feel we just don't measure up to. A worrying trend in self-esteem among teenage girls was highlighted in a major survey of 30,000 school pupils. In 2007, 41% of 14/15-year-old girls reported feeling high self-esteem. But that figure had dropped by 2014 to 33%.[1] As pressure to pursue the perfect image grows, it's no surprise that self-esteem is falling.

Body matters

As Christians, we can easily fall into the trap of being driven by a relentless pursuit of the body beautiful, either trying to attain it for ourselves or looking for it in someone else. But how should we react to a culture that worships perfect looks? Should we perhaps forget about our bodies and just focus on spiritual things? Maybe this is the 'holy grail' of finding satisfaction in Christ?

It's worth taking a moment to consider if our view of the body is in line with biblical thinking.

Mistakes we make
Body as idol
One error we make is to focus on our physical appearance to such an extent that it becomes a god. So we worry about whether or not we're good-looking. Or we become so obsessive about our gym routines, or exercise classes, or what

we wear, or our hair, or our complexion, that God stops being number one. Although keeping fit and healthy and taking care of our appearance are good things, we need to guard against making an idol of the body.

Body as worthless

And there's a more subtle, but equally dangerous, error. Rather than worshipping our bodies, we can treat them as worthless or bad, so that what we do with them is inconsequential. This belief that the spirit is good but matter is evil has its roots in the teachings of certain Greek philosophers. But we're taught in Genesis that after God had created everything, including man and woman with their physical bodies, he looked and saw that everything was 'very good' (1:31).

This disregard of the body can manifest itself in different ways. Some in the early church, for example, thought that whom they had sex with was unimportant. It was merely a physical act, an appetite to be satisfied, that didn't affect their spirit. This way of thinking is still prevalent today. Some people believe that we're going to die anyway, so we may as well have as much fun, including as much sex, as possible. The apostle Paul challenges this idea of separating body and soul: 'The body, however, is not meant for sexual immorality but for the Lord, and the Lord for the body' (1 Corinthians 6:13).

Body as pollutant

Another closely related error is to view the body from a 'super-spiritual' perspective as a potential pollutant to true spirituality. My friend Graham believes he can only be truly holy when he abstains from having sex with his wife. In his view, the physical act of sexual intercourse, even within marriage, defiles his pure spiritual worship.

Once again the apostle Paul counteracts this way of thinking, even though he teaches that abstaining from sexual relations for a certain period and for a stipulated purpose can have spiritual value. So he commands married people 'not [to] deprive each other except perhaps by mutual consent and for a time, so that you may devote yourselves to prayer. Then come together again so that Satan will not tempt you because of your lack of self-control' (1 Corinthians 7:5).

As Christians, we should not separate the physical from the spiritual in our thinking. We mustn't view our bodies as somehow less important (or even evil), and think that only 'spiritual things' really count or have value before God. No, my body and what I do with it really does matter.

Radical worship

I imagine that most of us have our own pet hates in church services. One of mine is hearing phrases like: 'Now we're going to have a time of worship', or 'Wasn't the worship great this morning?', or 'I just wish there was more worship.' When people say things like that, the word 'worship' usually means singing. But if you really want to annoy me, just announce that 'When we've *finished* worshipping God, Alan will read God's word for us before the minister comes to preach.' Aargh! I think I'd better explain . . .

My aversion to 'times of worship' is definitely not, as my friend Rebecca jokes, because I'm a grumpy old man (although, admittedly, I sometimes can be). But no, I abso-lutely love worshipping God in song. And not just the old hymns I grew up with either. I love singing all kinds of Christian music: old and new – psalms, hymns and spiritual songs – accompanied by all types of instruments, ancient and modern.

No, my problem is that to equate worship simply to a time of singing, no matter how joyful and uplifting, risks denigrating the biblical meaning of worship. Yes, of course we can worship God by singing – though we ought also to worship him by humbly listening to his word being read and preached – but true worship goes way beyond the confines of what takes place in a church service:

> Therefore, I urge you, brothers and sisters, in view of God's mercy, to offer your bodies as a living sacrifice, holy and pleasing to God – this is your true and proper worship. Do not conform to the pattern of this world, but be transformed by the renewing of your mind. Then you will be able to test and approve what God's will is – his good, pleasing and perfect will.
> (Romans 12:1–2)

So 'true and proper worship', according to Paul, is 'to offer [our] bodies as a living sacrifice, holy and pleasing to God', and we're to do this 'in view of God's mercy'. Paul sets out the wonders of God's mercy in the first eleven chapters of Romans. This mercy is seen primarily through the sacrifice of Jesus on the cross, by which he rescues us from sin and reconciles us to himself.

It's in light of this incredible act that Paul now urges Christians to offer our bodies as a living sacrifice. We saw earlier that God wants us to worship him with all our heart, soul and mind. But he wants my body too. True worship involves not only my inner self, but also my whole body.

In speaking about a living sacrifice, Paul is using Old Testament terminology. We can picture perhaps a bull, a sheep or a goat being handed over to the priest, who then cuts its throat and pours out its blood over the altar. We might well ask, what relevance does this have for us today? To many twenty-first-century ears, this may sound like a rather unseemly and messy business. But it still has relevance today.

Behaviour over beauty

Among the criteria for sacrificial offerings in Old Testament times was a stipulation that an animal must be unblemished. So you couldn't just use it as a convenient opportunity to quietly offload that bull with foot-and-mouth disease, or Larry the lamb with a dodgy eye. No, 'If the offering is a burnt offering from the herd, you are to offer a male without defect' (Leviticus 1:3). And 'If the offering is a burnt offering from the flock, from either the sheep or the goats, you are to offer a male without defect' (Leviticus 1:10).

With this requirement for perfection in mind, we may well ask, 'Why on earth would God want *my* body?' You might have acne, blotchy skin, wrinkles or a birthmark. You might be overweight or underweight. You might be long-sighted, short-sighted or hard of hearing, have a physical disability, a chronic disease or a terminal illness. Your body might always be tired, achy or fragile. Or perhaps it's generally in good working order, but you just don't like the way you look; you feel unattractive or physically awkward. Come to think of it, which of us has a body without a single blemish or defect that we can offer to God?

If you have a downer on your body, for whatever reason, then there's great news: God is not looking for physical perfection. He does not demand a body without defects, because the sacrifice of our bodies is not a sacrifice for sin. There's nothing you or I can do, or bring, that can add to or improve the perfect sacrifice of Jesus Christ. Even the acceptability of his supreme sacrifice was not because Jesus had perfect looks, of course:

> He had no beauty or majesty to attract us to him,
>   nothing in his appearance that we should desire him.
> (Isaiah 53:2)

Jesus was perfect because he was without sin.

So, if God does not want our bodies as a sacrifice for sin, what does he want them for? True and proper worship is to offer our bodies in a life of practical mercy towards other people. Paul goes on to demonstrate this in the remainder of Romans 12: God wants us to make the beauty of Jesus Christ visible through our bodies. So we're to use the gifts God has given us to serve others (verses 6–8), to be devoted to one another in love (verse 10), to share with the Lord's people who are in need, and practise hospitality (verse 13), and be careful to do what is right in the eyes of everyone (verse 17).

Jesus was perfect because he was without sin.

God is interested not in the physical beauty, but rather in the behaviour, of your body. My living sacrifice is not to offer bodily looks, but rather bodily behaviour. So forget the perfectly toned body with a six-pack, curves in all the right places and the gorgeous sun-kissed complexion.

Yes, of course we should look after ourselves physically and aim to stay healthy. But we must swim against the cultural tide and resist the temptation to worship our bodies. Instead, they're to be laid down and used as a vehicle with which to worship Christ and serve others.

Instruments of righteousness

Kofi came to me for support and advice concerning an addiction to pornography. Since he was eleven he'd regularly spent anything between three and four hours a night online, lusting over pornographic videos of men. Now, aged twenty-four, he would sometimes stay up through the night in an unceasing search for that perfect video. He would then drive into work having not slept at all. His addiction had ruined his social life and turned him into a virtual recluse. I listened to Kofi's story and asked the occasional question. I wanted to try to understand what underlying factors might be contributing to his behaviour.

One thing soon became apparent. Kofi had a terribly poor self-image. He hated his body. As a child, he'd been classed as 'clinically obese', and his weight had been the cause of some particularly nasty bullying. By mid-teens he was so distressed by the emotional and physical abuse that he committed himself to a radical regime of diet and exercise. I would never have guessed that he had been obese as a child, because Kofi was now healthy-looking and trim. But he couldn't see it at all. He still saw himself as the overweight, bullied child.

I wasn't surprised to learn that Kofi was only ever attracted to toned, gym-fit men. He couldn't bear to look at images or videos of any man whom he perceived to be even slightly overweight or out of shape. His pornography addiction seemed to be partially fuelled by a pursuit of the perfect body. And as he didn't believe he could ever attain this himself, he was driven to look for it in someone else.

Right thinking about the body was one of the keys to Kofi eventually breaking free of his addictive behaviour. I encouraged him to meditate on Psalm 139. He began to see himself as lovingly created by God, knit together in his mother's womb, fearfully and wonderfully made (Psalm 139:13–14). He stopped seeing the overweight, taunted child of his painful past. Even if he were still overweight, I assured him, God would still fully love and accept him in Christ.

Over time, Kofi stopped looking at porn and started using his body as a vehicle with which to worship God by showing mercy to others. He began by offering elderly people lifts to and from his church. He's now actively involved in church life.

Kofi found these words from earlier in Paul's letter to the Romans particularly challenging and helpful:

> Do not offer any part of yourself to sin as an instrument of wickedness, but rather offer yourselves to God as those who have been brought from death to life; and offer every part of yourself to him as an instrument of righteousness.
> (Romans 6:13)

Those verses should challenge all of us. Will I offer my body, not just in very general terms, but every individual part to God as a living sacrifice? How about my index finger, for example? As it clicks on the keyboard or mouse, or swipes across the screen of my smartphone or tablet, am I using it with evil intent, or offering it to God as an instrument of righteousness?

Self-image showdown: Rob's story

The specialist had told me there was every possibility I could be totally crippled by arthritis within three years if the medication didn't work. One morning, a few weeks after the diagnosis, I vividly remember being in so much pain that I couldn't even dress myself. Later my mum poured some cereal into a bowl for me, but I couldn't even grip the spoon to eat it. Things would get much worse though. I was devastated to be told that I had to stop playing football. I was also off work for months and lost my job. How bad could things get? In those first few months, as the medication was gradually taking effect, I strangely had an enormous sense of peace. My relationship with Jesus was becoming more precious than ever before.

Having wrestled with the question of whether God might be judging and punishing me for acting on my same-sex desires, I searched the Scriptures for a biblical perspective on suffering.

Job suffered despite being 'blameless and upright' (Job 1:1). Now, clearly, I hadn't lived a blameless and upright life (far from it!). But Jesus taught that the man born blind was not suffering the consequences of either his own, or his parents', sin (John 9:3). And as Christians, we can all be assured that 'the punishment that brought us peace was on him' (Isaiah 53:5). If Jesus has already taken the punishment for my sins, I can be confident that the God who is utterly just won't punish me for them too.

I did, however, come across a very helpful passage in Hebrews which speaks about God disciplining his children as would a perfect, loving father. The writer teaches Christians to 'endure hardship as discipline' (Hebrews 12:7), without encouraging us to draw lines and links between individual hardships and particular sins we might have committed. Well, I was enduring hardship in my body, so now it was a case of learning to accept this as God's training for righteous living.

God now challenged me to offer my body over to him. A showdown with my negative self-image kick-started this process. As I read God's word, I pondered how lavishly he must love me, to send his Son to die for me. I remember reading, 'But God demonstrates his own love for us in this: while we were still sinners, Christ died for us' (Romans 5:8).

As I reflected on the lengths God went to in order to rescue me, the Holy Spirit worked to transform my thinking and renew my mind. I began to think more positively about my self-image. God wanted me to use my body not for sexual immorality, but to serve others.

My poor self-image can still sometimes raise its ugly head (excuse pun). But step by step I'm learning that God accepts me just the way I am. And that he simply wants me to submit my imperfect body to be used in his service.

Since taking action to turn away from past habits and sinful acts, I've been amazed at some of the opportunities God has opened up for me to use parts of my body as instruments of righteousness. So, for example, I've been able to use my mouth to preach God's word and share my testimony. And my hands to help Jonathan write this book.

I passionately believe the promise that God works *all* things together for good for those who love him (Romans 8:28). And I've certainly experienced God working for good through my chronic illness. As my body weakens and as I cope with daily pain in my joints, it reminds me that time in this world is short. I can't waste my life. I will only live it to the full if I'm fully devoted to Jesus Christ, not just spiritually, but with my whole body too.

Thankfully, as we're about to see, we belong to the God who delights in using human weakness – physical, emotional or spiritual – to accomplish his great purposes. Purposes for our lives, for the lives of other people, for whole communities, or even nations. The Holy Spirit loves to enable those who are willing to trust not in their own resources, but in God's incomparable power.

9. USEFUL TO THE MASTER

For we are God's handiwork, created in Christ Jesus to
do good works, which God prepared in advance for us to do.
(Ephesians 2:10)

Delighting in weaknesses

Imagine the apostle Paul being introduced as the main speaker at a major international Christian conference today:

> We're delighted to have none other than the apostle Paul with us as our keynote speaker. He's written some pretty weighty and forceful letters, but in person he is unimpressive, and his speaking amounts to nothing. He has a thorn in his flesh, from which he hasn't been healed. He's frequently been imprisoned, beaten with rods three times, whipped five times, pelted with stones, often goes without food and sleep, and is constantly in danger. And I wouldn't ever go sailing with him, because he's already been shipwrecked three times. So give a big hand, please, as we welcome to the stage the incredibly weak apostle Paul.[1]

(Cue: slow hand clapping)

I don't know about you, but I've never heard a Christian speaker introduced in that way before. Normally, we tend to build people up. We focus on their qualifications, the letters after their names, their great achievements, the number of books they've written, or the size and 'success' of their church or ministry.

But Paul wasn't focused on such things. He delighted in his weaknesses. In fact, he recognized that being weak served God's purposes for his life. Paul recounts how, in order to keep him from becoming conceited (because of some great revelations he'd received), he was given a thorn in his flesh to torment him. He describes it as 'a messenger of Satan' (2 Corinthians 12:7), and pleads with the Lord three times to take this thorn away. Notice how God answers him:

> But he said to me, 'My grace is sufficient for you, for my power is made perfect in weakness.' Therefore I will boast all the more gladly about my weaknesses, so that Christ's power may rest on me. That is why, for Christ's sake, I delight in weaknesses, in insults, in hardships, in persecutions, in difficulties. For when I am weak, then I am strong.
> (2 Corinthians 12:9–10)

Undervalued commodity

In God's economy, human weakness is immensely valuable: 'Weakness, with acknowledgement of it, is the fittest seat and subject for God to perfect his strength in; for consciousness of our infirmities drives us out of ourselves to him in whom our strength lies',[2] according to the Puritan Richard Sibbes.

If we're willing to delight in our weaknesses, struggles, sufferings and trials, we pave the way for Christ's power to rest on us and work through us. But we should be under no illusion: this is completely counter-cultural. Weakness is not generally considered as a precious commodity in our society. Tragically, it's not always highly valued in evangelical circles either. But a local church that recognizes the value of 'weak' people, especially the marginalized and alienated, is a church much more likely to experience the power of the Holy Spirit at work.

Twenty-eight-year-old Greg had experienced same-sex attractions since childhood. By God's grace, he'd never once acted on his desires, and was fully committed to living a life of sexual purity. God had evidently entrusted to him a particular gift for teaching the Bible and modelling the Christian life to younger people. He had been the youth worker in a large evangelical church, and was universally loved and respected by the young people and their parents alike. That is, until word got out that he was attracted to the same sex.

Suddenly Greg was *persona non grata* within his own church family. He had never felt even a hint of attraction to teenage boys. But his weakness of struggling with same-sex temptations apparently now disqualified him from youth work and made him a 'danger to young people'. Naturally, he was devastated.

Worse than rubbish

Your CV does not impress God. This includes which school, college or university you attended, or the grades you achieved. He is not impressed by your employment history, your accomplishments at work, or by any promotions or commendations you've earned. Forget your voluntary work, sporting prowess, musical gifts or other talents, or any awards or medals you've won. He's not impressed by your Bible knowledge, prayer life, godliness, or by your Christian service, however faithful and tireless.

Whatever our family, friends, peers and colleagues find most striking and inspiring about our lives, we can all be assured that God is simply not impressed.

Paul had an enviable CV. Certainly as far as religious pedigree was concerned, he had good reason to be highly confident, because he had it all:

> If someone else thinks they have reasons to put confidence in the flesh, I have more: circumcised on the eighth day, of the people of Israel, of the tribe of Benjamin, a Hebrew of Hebrews; in regard to the law, a Pharisee; as for zeal, persecuting the church; as for righteousness based on the law, faultless.
>
> (Philippians 3:4–6)

But compared to the 'surpassing worth of knowing Christ Jesus my Lord', Paul considers all of these other things as 'garbage' (verse 8). Now garbage is a rather polite translation of the Greek. The shock value of what Paul writes is perhaps better captured in the older King James Version, which opts for the somewhat bolder English word: 'dung'. So, compared to knowing Christ Jesus, Paul considers everything else that he used to trust and put his confidence in as utterly worthless, disgusting, smelly dung.

Why then is God not bowled over by the kinds of things that tend to impress our contemporaries? Put simply, it's because God hates human boasting, unless we're boasting in him. If we're trusting in our brilliant CV, our personal achievements, our moral standing or in anything other than the cross of Jesus Christ, we'll inevitably exalt ourselves rather than glorify God.

Better boasting

Despite being described as more humble than anyone else on the face of the earth, Moses' downfall was pride. To protect themselves, Abraham and Sarai failed to trust God and lied about the nature of their relationship. Jacob deceived his father to obtain the blessing due to his brother Esau. David, the man after God's own heart, committed adultery and murdered his mistress's husband. Peter, despite assuring Jesus he'd lay down his life for him, went on to deny him three times. Great men and women of God, but each one fallible and imperfect.

As we read the Bible, it's clear that throughout history, God has been pleased to use all kinds of people in his service, but especially those who are weak, with flawed characters. This should not surprise us. Even today God remains in the business of choosing weak people whom the world often rejects and looks down upon:

> Brothers and sisters, think of what you were when you were called. Not many of you were wise by human standards; not many were influential; not many were of noble birth. But God chose the foolish things of the world to shame the wise; God chose the weak things of the world to shame the strong. God chose the lowly things of this world and the despised things – and the things that are not – to nullify the things that are, so that no one may boast before him.
> (1 Corinthians 1:26–29)

Testing my heart

'It's a question of discerning God's timing, Jonathan. We're thinking when, not if.'

I took this as a gentle hint from my pastor that the answer from the church's Mission Council meeting the next evening was likely to be a 'no'. Or more accurately a 'not yet'. I believed God was calling me to be a minister of the gospel. Perhaps it would be as a pastor or as a missionary – I really wasn't sure. The details were far from clear. But I had a deep love for God's word and a growing conviction that he was preparing me to teach and preach it to other people.

The church leaders rightly wanted to test my sense of calling, and had advised me to apply to the Mission Council. If they agreed that I demonstrated the necessary gifting, character and spiritual maturity, then I could be formally supported by the church for ministry training at Bible college.

I'd initially protested when the process was explained to me. I queried whether training was really necessary, as, after all, weren't both Peter and John 'unschooled, ordinary men' (Acts 4:13)? Even after five years as a Christian my zeal wasn't always matched by wisdom and humility. But the greater concern of the church leaders was whether I was able to demonstrate consistency in godly living. I was still potentially vulnerable to falling back into a pattern of same-sex practice, or of developing emotionally over-dependent friendships.

God, it seemed, shared their concerns. And throughout the next day it felt like he was testing what was in my heart. I faced a barrage of temptations. Some were subtle, like a sudden urge to look at pornography, which hadn't troubled me for many months. Others seemed to be directly from Satan, and were more blatant. Such as Jack (see chapter 6) – whom I hadn't seen or heard from for nearly two years now – turning up unannounced at my flat on the pretext of missing me and wanting to chat.

But whatever the temptation, the Holy Spirit seemed to strengthen me inwardly. One after another, Bible verses tumbled into my mind: 'Resist the devil, and he will flee from you' (James 4:7); 'God is faithful; he will not let you be tempted beyond what you can bear' (1 Corinthians 10:13); 'Be alert and of sober mind . . . Resist him, standing firm in the faith' (1 Peter 5:8–9).

My times in his hands

By God's grace I did stand firm, although I turned up for the interview with the Mission Council feeling battle-weary and weak. I was prepared to concede that I was indeed still vulnerable and not yet ready to train for Christian ministry. But even so, I shared with the five-person panel how I believed God had been leading and equipping me for some kind of future ministry. I explained how a few weeks earlier I'd heard a preacher, Alistair Begg, teaching from 2 Timothy at a weekend conference in Dorset on the theme: 'Useful to the Master'. And how my heart had been strangely gripped by God's word and by a deep conviction that God wanted me to preach and teach this same word to others.

After nearly three hours of gracious, yet probing, questioning, serious discussion and earnest prayer, I was asked to wait outside as they reached their decision. It seemed interminable, but eventually I was called back in.

'We believe God is calling you to vocational gospel ministry. We were intending to say "not yet" and encourage you to wait. But we're convinced beyond doubt that God is saying that now is the right time. We just cannot resist the Holy Spirit's leading. So it's a yes.'

That night I learnt, not for the first or the last time, that I belonged to the God who is pleased to work through human weakness, and whose perfect timing can always be trusted. My attendance at Bible college and my church placement were both marked out by ongoing weakness and frailty. As was my time as assistant pastor and youth worker at an evangelical church in London. And it wasn't because I suddenly became strong and invincible that the same church subsequently appointed me as their pastor.

Ironically, it was when I did begin to rely on my own strength and foolishly forget my personal weaknesses that things started to unravel for me. And God would soon have to remind me of my utter dependence on him.

Fit for purpose?

'My spirits were sunken so low that I could weep by the hour like a child, and yet I knew not what I wept for.'[3]

In addition to dark depression, Charles Spurgeon, known as the 'Prince of Preachers', also suffered from gout, rheumatism and kidney disease.

Charles Spurgeon, known as the 'Prince of Preachers', also suffered from gout, rheumatism and kidney disease.

'My witness,' he said in a lecture to students, 'is that those who are honoured of their Lord in public have usually to endure a secret chastening, or to carry a peculiar cross, lest by any means they exalt themselves and fall into the snare of the devil.'[4]

So you don't need to wait until you feel strong and physically fit before God can use you in his service. You and I have been created for the very purpose of doing good works that God himself has prepared in advance for us to do. 'We have different gifts, according to the grace given to each of us' (Romans 12:6). And by his power we can use our God-given gift or gifts to do those good works in the midst of weakness, or illness, or struggle, or suffering.

Now it's true, of course, that the more we devote ourselves to godly living, the more useful we become in God's service. Usefulness to the Master, as Paul explains, is inextricably linked to being 'made holy' (2 Timothy 2:21). And that involves God's servants turning away from wickedness (verse 19) and pursuing righteousness, faith, love and peace (verse 22).

But God does not want us to wait until we're free from trials, or perfectly holy (neither of which will happen until Christ returns), before we step out in faith to serve him and others.

Rechannelling the intractable

'I want to be useful to God, but first I need to sort myself out and find freedom from these same-sex attractions.'

Caroline was chatting to me at the end of a conference at which I'd been speaking. I had talked about how God uses us not just despite our weaknesses, but because of them. She fought back tears as she sat down. She was forty-five, married with two children, and evidently loved God. Caroline wasn't acting on her attractions, and was determined by God's grace not to do so. She just found it so hard to believe that God was ready to use her now, in the midst of all the emotional turmoil. That she didn't need to wait.

'But surely God won't want to use me yet?' she protested, 'not with all the dark desires and longings I'm battling with. You have no idea how rotten my heart is.'

She was partly right. I had no idea how rotten her heart was. But I did know my own heart pretty well. And I knew that my weaknesses and failings had never excluded me from serving God. Quite the opposite. Many times I'd been conscious of Christ's power working in and through me when I'd felt at the end of myself, with no human strength left.

Can God really use you in the midst of temptations and weaknesses? Can you, or someone you're supporting, be useful to the Master even in the midst of a struggle with same-sex temptations? The answer is an absolute, unequivocal yes. I'd dare to suggest that perhaps I've been more useful in God's service because of my struggle, as I have a daily reminder of my vulnerability and utter dependence on him.

Scottish pastor William Still suggests that those struggling with same-sex attraction should trust God, 'with a view to seeing how he will re-channel its desire, if intractable, towards something to be used by God', such as in 'loving relationships, especially in the befriending and helping of needy souls'.[5]

I would add, from personal experience, that the struggle can also be used by God to deepen our personal knowledge of him and to help our relationship with him flourish. Although, as I would soon have to learn, sometimes such growth comes through a dark night of the soul.

10. PURSUING INTIMACY WITH GOD

I thirst for you,
my whole being longs for you,
in a dry and parched land
where there is no water.
(Psalm 63:1)

Searching for meaning

'Intimacy is the capacity to be rather weird with someone – and finding that that's ok with them.'[1]

I smiled when I first read that quote. And I also wondered – if that's true – why don't I find it much easier to pursue intimacy with God and others? Because, as some of my friends could testify, being weird comes pretty naturally to me. But I guess those words were always intended as a playful observation, not as an authoritative definition.

So how do we define it? Intimacy is a difficult concept to pin down and explain. In our highly sexualized culture, the word is often reduced to mean physical touch, including sexual relations. And some people would assume that particular meaning if I were to say something like: 'Last night I spent an intimate evening with a friend.'

The noun doesn't appear in the more literal translations of the Bible, although there are several occurrences of the adjective 'intimate'. Job, for example, in the midst of his extreme suffering, exclaims,

All my intimate friends detest me;
    those I love have turned against me.
(Job 19:19)

Now, admittedly, that example will hardly inspire you to pursue intimacy. But later Job reminisces and cries out,

Oh, for the days when I was in my prime,
    when God's intimate friendship blessed my house.
(Job 29:4)

God's intimate friendship. That's more like it. Let's first think about intimacy in terms of friendship with God. The God who 'detests the perverse but takes the upright into his confidence' (Proverbs 3:32). Just imagine being taken into the confidence of Almighty God – wouldn't that be worth pursuing? (More about that later.) Let's go back to where it all began.

Mysterious blueprint

'In the beginning God . . .' The Bible opens with those four simple words. We then learn that 'the Spirit of God was hovering over the waters' (Genesis 1:2). Later we discover the Son of God was there at the outset too: 'In the beginning was the Word' (John 1:1), and 'The Word became flesh and made his dwelling among us . . . the glory of the one and only Son' (John 1:14).

So in all eternity, before a single thing was created, God simply 'is'. One God, three distinct persons – Father, Son and Holy Spirit. And as the biblical narrative unfolds, we learn that they have always been in an intimate relationship together. The Father loves the Son (John 5:20), and the Son loves the Father (John 14:31). Indeed, the Father is in the Son, and the Son is in the Father (John 17:21). The Spirit of God is also the Spirit of Christ (Romans 8:9). He listens to the Father (John 16:13) and glorifies the Son (John 16:14).

But the three persons of the Godhead not only enjoy intimate relationship together; they also collaborate to create the heavens and the earth. We know they work together because at the pinnacle of creation we get to eavesdrop on a brief heavenly conversation:

> Let *us* make mankind in *our* image, in *our* likeness, so that they may rule over the fish in the sea and the birds in the sky, over the livestock and all the wild animals, and over all the creatures that move along the ground.
> (Genesis 1:26, italics mine)

Now theologians have long debated precisely what it means for men and women to be created in the image of God. The verse above draws attention to the aspect of human rule over the world. God rules. Therefore we too, as bearers of the divine image, are to exercise delegated dominion over his creation. So the very first command God gives humankind includes the instruction to 'rule' (Genesis 1:28).

But there are many other implications of you and me being made in God's image. Not least that we're made as relational creatures. We have an inbuilt capacity, and a need, to relate and work together. Together with God, and also with other people too, as we'll see in the next chapter.

Our most important relationship of all, though, is with God. And, incredibly, he wants to draw people into this close-knit community of divine love between Father, Son and Spirit. To whomever loves Jesus and obeys his teaching, Jesus promises that both Father and Son (by the Spirit) 'will come to them and make our home with them' (John 14:23).

Background noise in the garden

Joshua put on his baseball cap and busked for around forty-five minutes during rush hour at a busy metro station, his violin case open for donations. But strangely enough, he wasn't in it for the money. Joshua Bell is one of America's finest musicians. A renowned violinist. And he was playing an instrument handcrafted by Antonio Stradivari in the 1700s – worth millions.

This unlikely urban concert was a social experiment initiated by the *Washington Post*. The premise was simple. Would commuters rushing to work 'recognize beauty in their midst'? The answer was no. The 'internationally acclaimed virtuoso' turned virtually no heads while playing six classical masterpieces. Approximately 1,097 people passed by. Just seven stopped to listen, and only one individual recognized him.[2]

Failing to appreciate beauty in our midst. I'm sure we're all guilty of it. And so were our ancestors whom we met earlier. Adam and Eve lived in a perfect and stunningly beautiful world. Perfect for a short while at least. In the beginning they enjoyed deep, sweet, uninterrupted and unblemished fellowship with their Creator. How amazing! I don't know about you, but I find that difficult even to imagine.

But after their attempted coup in the garden, everything changes. Their calamitous failure to resist temptation ruins their experience of God's presence. Now he's mere background noise to their ears:

> Then the man and his wife heard the sound of the LORD God as he was walking in the garden in the cool of the day, and they hid from the LORD God among the trees of the garden. But the LORD God called to the man, 'Where are you?'
> (Genesis 3:8)

What a tragedy! They 'heard the sound' of God walking. Previously, they'd walked and talked with him. They'd enjoyed perfect intimacy with the living God. Now the sound of his footsteps is the catalyst for a hurried game of hide-and-seek. Although they're not very good at it, like when I used to hide confidently behind the curtains as a boy, not realizing my feet were sticking out. So it doesn't take God long to find them.

But at least he *wants* to find them. God takes the initiative. He pursues them. For judgment initially, but mercy and restored relationship are also on his mind.

Stirring epitaph for Enoch

Writing an obituary is a tricky thing to do at the best of times. How can you even do justice to a whole life in a short newspaper column? And when the man in question lived for 365 years? Oh, and throw this into the mix: he didn't technically die; he just vanished: 'Enoch walked faithfully with God; then he was no more, because God took him away' (Genesis 5:24).

Adam and Eve are judged by God. He banishes them from the garden and bars the way to the Tree of Life. They no longer experience the close communion they once enjoyed. As a result of their disobedience, death enters the world, which is driven home by the refrain running through the genealogy of Genesis 5: 'then he died'.

But then we meet Enoch. And he didn't die. Instead, God 'took him away'. There was something very different about this man, something that gives us hope. Intimate relationship with God can be restored. In a fallen, broken world, Enoch walks with God. The metaphor suggests close and intimate fellowship, to such an extent that he's taken from this world and placed right into God's presence. There's a stirring mention of this in Hebrews:

> By faith Enoch was taken from this life, so that he did not experience death: 'He could not be found, because God had taken him away.' For before he was taken, he was commended as one who pleased God. And without faith it is impossible to please God, because anyone who comes to him must believe that he exists and that he rewards those who earnestly seek him. (Hebrews 11:5–6)

But I can't see God

Mike is in his thirties. He left his same-sex partner after becoming a Christian a few years ago. I got one of those quizzical looks from him again. I'd been explaining how I wouldn't want to exchange the intimacy I now have with Jesus for the intimacy that I used to have with my same-sex partner.

'I think I understand what you're saying, Jonathan, but I can't see God. My ex-partner was physically there, but God isn't.'

I knew exactly what he was getting at. And of course, he was right. We can't see God. And if we were to see God, we wouldn't live to tell the tale. Because as Moses was warned,

'You cannot see my face, for no one may see me and live' (Exodus 33:20).

Mike wakes up in the morning, prays and reads his Bible, but Jesus isn't physically in front of him. At church he worships the 'King eternal, immortal, invisible, the only God' (1 Timothy 1:17), but he can't physically see this eternal King who's invisible – because, well, he's invisible. By contrast, on an average day Mike sees many attractive men. And although he does his best to look away and not lust, it doesn't stop him from craving intimacy.

'I'm at that age where most of my friends are married. They have someone to share their whole life with. They can be physically close. And yes, I know I can enjoy intimate friendship with God. But God can't hug me.'

Mike's temptation is to pursue physical and emotional intimacy with attractive men whom he can see. But he tries to resist this in obedience to the God he can't see. I get it. I share the same struggle. At root, it's a question of faith. As we saw, Enoch was commended as one who pleased God, because he walked with him by faith.

At root, it's a question of faith.

But what is faith? According to the writer of Hebrews, it's 'confidence in what we hope for and assurance about what we do not see' (Hebrews 11:1). So the unavoidable reality is that, this side of heaven, our intimate walk with God is a relationship based on 'hope' and 'assurance' in a Saviour whom 'we do not see'.

Now, we can, of course, see our brothers and sisters in Christ. Does this perhaps hold out some hope for Mike in this life? (We'll explore this in the next chapter.)

Hibernation and revelation: Jonathan's story

I've never been a great sleeper. Even as a teenager, I'd invariably be awake and active by 7 am. And I'm talking here about weekends and school holidays (yes, I know, that's tragic, as my school friend Nicholas used to tell me).

But I'll always remember one period in my life when I slept well. Really well. So deeply, in fact, that I didn't want to get up in the mornings. Or in the afternoons. And sometimes not in the evenings either. If and when I did get up, I'd usually potter around for an hour or two before going back to bed and sleeping some more. During this whole period – nearly a year – I enjoyed the deepest, richest, most refreshing and reinvigorating sleep I've ever experienced.

True, my hibernation was occasionally pierced by a terrifying nightmare, which would wake me up in a cold sweat. But my doctor had warned about the potential side effects of the medication. And nightmares were at the lower end of the risk profile, after suicidal tendencies, hallucinations and paranoia. I remember asking myself if pills that could induce those kinds of effects were really the best remedy for someone signed off work with anxiety and depression. But I was too tired to worry about it. And anyway, it was time to get some more sleep.

Was it the pressure of pastoral ministry that caused my body and mind to down tools and stop working? Maybe. Or was it the fact that I'd lost sight of my personal relationship with God as the most important thing? Probably. Or was it perhaps because God was no longer truly number one in my life, as other people and things had surreptitiously taken his place on the throne of my heart? Certainly. Or could it simply have been a chemical reaction in my brain? Possibly.

The truth is that I don't know exactly what caused the anxiety and depression. Quite likely it was a combination of all of the above. But I am convinced that the Lord used it for good. When I look back, it seems that perhaps God had decided enough was enough. That he needed to remove me from the firing line of pastoral ministry and take me back to basics. To remind me that nothing was more precious than my relationship with him.

God seemed absent. For many months I was too exhausted to pray or read my Bible – and anyway, what was the point? I felt hopeless and fearful for the future, particularly as it was becoming apparent that I couldn't contemplate returning to my pastoral role at the church. Everything that had been important to me was slowly stripped away until I was left with God. God alone. The God whom I just didn't seem able to – or even want to – reconnect with.

The Lord confides in those who fear him

But it was at this darkest, lowest point in my depression that the Lord himself took the initiative. He broke in. He pursued me, even though I'd stopped desiring him. One night I awoke suddenly with a strong urge to read the Bible. I turned to the Psalms, and verse after verse came alive. It was as if the Holy Spirit were freely pouring the soothing honey of God's truth over my bruised soul. One psalm, in particular, pierced my heart:

> The LORD confides in those who fear him;
>> he makes his covenant known to them.
> My eyes are ever on the LORD,
>> for only he will release my feet from the snare.
> (Psalm 25:14–15)

I can count my really close, intimate friends on one hand. With them I'm willing to confide and share the innermost secrets of my heart. I have no fear of being vulnerable (or weird) with them. And it's mutual. This, for me, is one of the marks of true friendship, as distinguished from 'mates' or mere acquaintances.

And it's this level of intimacy that God desires to have with you and me. He wants to be your intimate friend. To take you into his confidence and share what's on his heart. And there's just one condition: you must 'fear him'. God wants you to take your friendship with him really seriously, to revere and honour him in your heart and through your behaviour. This was one of the key lessons I learnt through being laid aside with depression.

The Lord Jesus offered this same level of intimacy to his disciples. Notice how he confided in them:

> Greater love has no one than this: to lay down one's life for one's friends. You are my friends if you do what I command. I no longer call you servants, because a servant does not know his master's business. Instead, I have called you friends, for everything that I learned from my Father I have made known to you.
> (John 15:13–15)

Building deep friendship with the invisible God

Let's get practical. How can same-sex attracted Christians build intimacy with God? And how can we be better equipped to resist same-sex temptations through a growing relationship with God?

Here are four principles that I find helpful, both personally and in supporting others:

1. Be single-minded

I'm often in two minds. About what to do on my day off, what to cook (or more likely microwave) for dinner, whether

I can be bothered to exercise or not – mostly trivial things. But in our relationship with God, being double-minded is a serious business, as the prophet Elijah made clear to Israel: 'Elijah went before the people and said, "How long will you waver between two opinions? If the LORD is God, follow him; but if Baal is God, follow him"' (1 Kings 18:21).

The worship of the false god Baal is not my temptation, and I imagine it's not yours either. But I am rather skilled in wavering between two opinions, and, especially when same-sex temptations rage, not always quick to follow the Lord. I too easily allow myself little indulgences: a casual lustful glance, or replaying the memory of a past sinful act. Relatively minor compromises you might think. But they have a cumulative effect, and subtly lead me into greater temptations. So on occasions the Holy Spirit has had to convict me to make a decisive break with the past.

I don't know what this might involve for you, or for someone you support. Deleting certain photos or emails, perhaps. Or purging details of old contacts from your phone, shutting down a fake Skype account or blocking access to unhelpful websites. Maybe avoiding certain places, people or situations. Be ruthless! A Christian friend recently deleted his Facebook account after 'people you may know' started to throw up certain men from his past life even though he'd never even given those men his real name.

'Blessed are the pure in heart,' says Jesus, 'for they will see God' (Matthew 5:8). If I'm genuinely committed to pursuing an intimate friendship with God, I need to stop wavering, make up my mind, and follow him as my number one. To delight in Jesus as the ultimate satisfier of my heart. I find this prayer helpful when I'm in two minds about my devotion to God:

Teach me your way, LORD,
>   that I may rely on your faithfulness;
> give me an undivided heart,
>   that I may fear your name.
> (Psalm 86:11)

2. Worship with reality

'How's it going?'

>   'Good, thanks. You?'

>   'I'm fine, thanks.'

>   'Great . . .'

If you're a Christian, you've probably had a conversation like this at church. To my shame, I've participated in many similar ones. We may fool others into thinking we're 'fine', but we belong to the God who searches the heart and examines the mind (Jeremiah 17:10). It's impossible to hide from God the truth of where we're at in our relationship with him. So why not simply be real with him in worship and prayer?

Israel's songbook, the Psalms, is packed full of raw emotion. The songwriters are completely honest with God. They pour out their hearts and tell him exactly how they feel. Their expressions of lament are usually followed by intense declarations of praise and trust in God. But the psalmists only reach this place of confidence as they share their pain, frustration, disappointment, fear and anxiety.

> How long, LORD? Will you forget me for ever?
>   How long will you hide your face from me?
> How long must I wrestle with my thoughts
>   and day after day have sorrow in my heart?
> How long will my enemy triumph over me?
> (Psalm 13:1–2)

Despair. But then, just a few verses later, the psalmist confidently declares,

> But I trust in your unfailing love;
>   my heart rejoices in your salvation.
> I will sing the LORD's praise,
>   for he has been good to me.
> (verses 5–6)

The Lord is not detached from what we're going through. He's right here with us. By his Spirit, he's actually *in* us. And one of the best ways to grow in intimacy with God is to involve him in our struggles by expressing what we're feeling in worship and prayer. Sometimes that might mean admitting that you're enslaved to a particular sin and can't break free. Maybe you don't even have the desire to break free. If that's the case, then praying, 'Lord, please take away the love of sinning' would be a great starting place. God longs for reality from his children.

3. Revel in the goodness of God

Miserable, lonely, distraught, frustrated, depressed, wretched. Words that some people have used to describe to me their experience of denying themselves a same-sex relationship. They do it because they love Jesus Christ and passionately believe he says no. However, it can leave some feeling that God is far from good.

But the truth that God is good is asserted robustly throughout the Bible. 'The LORD is upright,' declares the psalmist; 'he is my Rock, and there is no wickedness in him' (Psalm 92:15). 'Give thanks to the LORD, for he is good; his love endures for ever,' the priests are instructed to declare before the Ark of God (1 Chronicles 16:34).

Believing that the Lord is good is fine in theory. But how can we revel, or take intense delight, in his goodness when he says no to something that we might feel is good and desirable? Or if we don't appear to be experiencing good things?

Well, it's important to recognize first that there can be all kinds of reasons why we may not feel as if we're experiencing the goodness of God. Sometimes it may be down to physical tiredness, sickness or emotional exhaustion. Or I might be isolating myself (or becoming isolated by circumstances) from other believers – and God often reveals his goodness through others, or uses the words of others to encourage us to recognize the good things he gives us in Christ. So it's certainly worth considering if any of those factors may be affecting my sense of spiritual well-being and, wherever possible, taking remedial action.

Fundamentally, though, close relationships are built on trust. And that's no less the case for developing an intimate friendship with the living God. So begin perhaps by asking God for faith to believe that genuine joy is found only by submitting to his perfect will. And faith to accept that any pleasure found outside of Christ's will is deceitful, temporary and ultimately unsatisfying.

We have to take God at his word.

We have to take God at his word. To trust that he is good and rewards those who earnestly seek him, even if our circumstances and emotions might tempt us to doubt his goodness. When I was suffering from depression, a trusted friend encouraged me with this verse:

> Who among you fears the LORD
>   and obeys the word of his servant?

Let the one who walks in the dark,
  who has no light,
trust in the name of the LORD
  and rely on their God.
(Isaiah 50:10)

4. Listen attentively

If I reflect on my handful of close and intimate friendships, one common thread stands out. The people I'm closest to, and trust most, are, without exception, those to whom I've devoted the most time, energy and passion in getting to know. I've asked questions, listened carefully to the answers (mostly!), and fully committed myself to understanding what makes them tick.

That may not sound like an earth-shattering observation. But it's worth asking, am I doing the same in my relationship with God? Am I devoting time, energy and passion in getting to know the Father, Son and Holy Spirit? Am I asking lots of questions, listening carefully to the answers, and genuinely desiring to know who God is, what's on his heart, and how he wants me to live?

We conceded earlier that we can't see God. But we can hear him. In contrast to dumb idols, our God speaks. His breathed-out words in the Bible are useful for teaching us, rebuking us, correcting us, and training us how to live a life that pleases him (2 Timothy 3:16). And his words are alive and active: they cut to the heart with the sharpness of a double-edged sword, judging our deepest thoughts and attitudes (Hebrews 4:12).

Psalm 19 gives further motivation to listen attentively to, and feed on, God's perfect word, which:

- refreshes the soul (verse 7a)
- makes simple people wise (verse 7b)

- gives joy to the heart (verse 8a)
- gives light to the eyes (verse 8b)
- is firm and good (verse 9)
- is more precious than gold (verse 10a)
- is sweeter than the honeycomb (verse 10b)
- warns (verse 11a)
- brings great reward (verse 11b).

Our God still speaks today. God has a word for you that is authoritative, utterly dependable, unchanging and without error. If we're serious about building an intimate friendship with him, then we need to devote time and energy to this relationship. We will only get to know God better as we listen to his word in the Bible, including the challenging truths about sex and relationships. And getting to know God better is so important. Because, note this, the depth of our relationships with other people is inextricably linked to the depth of our relationship with God.

11. ENJOYING INTIMACY WITH OTHERS

Now that you have purified yourselves by obeying the
truth so that you have sincere love for each other,
love one another deeply, from the heart.
(1 Peter 1:22)

Looking for a helper

'But didn't God say it's not good for us to be alone? So surely it's not good for a same-sex attracted Christian to be on their own? I need a partner, someone to share my life with. Someone who'll be there for me if things fall apart.'

Helen looked me straight in the eye. She was angry. Angry with God. She was in her final year at university studying pharmacy. Brought up in the faith by loving parents, a keen Christian, passionate about sharing the gospel and President of her CU. But she was also desperate for a partner.

'God did say that it's not good for mankind to be alone,' I replied, 'but the context is important. Let's look at Genesis together.'

We skim-read Genesis 1 and see a refrain running through the chapter. At various stages of creation the narrator comments, 'And God saw that it was good' (verses 10, 12, 18, 21 and 25). After making mankind in his own image (verse 27), we note how 'God saw all that he had made, and it was very good' (verse 31).

But then, into the context of a very good creation, God springs a surprise: 'The LORD God said, "It is not good for the man to be alone. I will make a helper suitable for him"' (Genesis 2:18).

This is fascinating. Before the fall, God highlights something 'not good' in creation. At this point sin hasn't yet entered the world. So not good means incomplete rather than intrinsically evil. And there's something else worth noting. Having recognized that it's not good for Adam to be alone, you might imagine that God would want to make him a companion. But instead he makes him 'a helper'. Why?

Loneliness or aloneness?

I got myself in trouble some years ago, after speaking from Genesis 1 – 3 at a conference in Minnesota, USA, when a young journalist tore me to shreds for, apparently, ranting about creation. But that wasn't the worst bit. He also made a comment to the effect that Jonathan wonders why he doesn't have a wife. (I don't wonder.) He'll never be married, though, said the journalist, because he thinks women are created merely as men's helpers.

Now before we lose all our female readers, please be assured that that is *not* what I said at the conference, and it is not even close to what I believe! Nor do I think 'helping' is sufficient to define the essence of marriage. As we saw earlier, Jesus has a high view of marriage as a permanent, one-flesh union between a man and a woman. But we can't escape the fact that God determines to make a helper for Adam. And importantly, in no sense is this a derogatory term. The same root word in Hebrew describes God himself, for example, as 'our *help* and our shield' (Psalm 33:20). We find a useful clue as to why a helper is needed a few verses earlier: 'The LORD God took the man and put him in the Garden of Eden to work it and take care of it' (Genesis 2:15).

So the fundamental problem in Genesis 2:18, it seems, is not Adam's emotional and physical loneliness. Rather, it's his aloneness in working the garden. There's so much work to be done. Too much for one man to do on his own. He needs a helper. And marriage will become the means to create additional 'helpers' too, so humankind can fulfil God's command to 'Be fruitful and increase in number; fill the earth and subdue it' (Genesis 1:28).

But why is this so important? Well, because in church we sometimes speak about marriage as the solution to loneliness or singleness (which presupposes that singleness is a problem needing to be solved). Or some believe that marriage is the only context in which Christians can experience deep love and godly intimacy.

As Helen and I looked at Genesis, the anger in her eyes started to melt away. She seemed intrigued. She even spoke with cautious excitement in her voice.

'So you're saying that in Genesis 2:18 human loneliness or the lack of a companion is not really the problem that God sets out to solve?'

'I believe that's what the text suggests,' I answered.

'Hmm, OK. That's very interesting.' It was like a light had been switched on.

Captured by a better vision

'Lovers are normally face to face, absorbed in each other; friends, side by side, absorbed in some common interest.'[1]

Those words of C. S. Lewis provide a helpful insight into enjoying intimacy with others. Close friends are usually united by, and focused on, a mutual interest or interests, preoccupied with something other than their friendship. This is not to say there isn't a place for celebrating a close friendship, or indulging in 'deep and meaningful' chats, or for those precious moments when we just enjoy being with a trusted friend. But I've certainly learnt, through costly trial and error, that godly intimacy tends to flourish best when the friendship itself is not the primary focus.

There are many things that we may have in common with our friends. Rob and I both love football (though I support Arsenal, and Rob – despite much persuading – insists on supporting Man Utd). Football may not be your thing, but with your friends you might appreciate the same kind of music, books, TV series or films. Or maybe your shared interest is cooking, chess, walking, cycling, travelling, gaming or the theatre.

With other believers, of course, we have (or should have) a more obvious mutual interest. We're united by the gospel of Jesus Christ, and by a love for Christ himself. In the light of our unity with Christ, Paul urges Christians to be 'like-minded, having the same love, being one in spirit and of one mind' (Philippians 2:2). So surely an excellent way to nurture godly intimacy is to have the Lord Jesus as both the foundation for, and primary focus of, a friendship (or indeed of a marriage).

Together for the gospel

Have you ever considered why Jesus sent out his disciples two by two? 'Calling the Twelve to him, he began to send them out two by two and gave them authority over impure spirits' (Mark 6:7); 'After this the Lord appointed seventy-two others and sent them two by two ahead of him to every town and place where he was about to go' (Luke 10:1).

Judging by what Jesus told the seventy-two next, it might seem counterproductive: 'The harvest is plentiful, but the workers are few. Ask the Lord of the harvest, therefore, to send out workers into his harvest field' (Luke 10:2).

Logic tells us that more could have been done had the seventy-two gone out individually. Surely this would have been a much better use of resources? Double the hands to reap double the harvest. We're not told why Jesus sends them out in pairs, and there could be multiple reasons. But I'll offer some (hopefully) sanctified speculation. Could it be, knowing that the work would be difficult, that Jesus had Genesis 2:18 in mind and didn't think it would be good for them to serve alone?

Paul certainly felt alone at times in his ministry (see 2 Timothy 1:15; 4:10, 16). He was, of course, an unmarried man. But you don't get the general impression from Paul's letters of a lonely man living a sad, unfulfilled life. Quite the opposite. He passionately served and proclaimed Christ as Lord. And he saw the value of serving God alongside others too, often forming strong and intimate bonds with his friends and co-workers. Notice how he writes about them with real warmth and affection:

Epaphras: 'our dear fellow servant . . . a faithful minister of Christ on our behalf' (Colossians 1:7).

Luke: 'our dear friend' (Colossians 4:14).

Onesiphorus: 'he often refreshed me' (2 Timothy 1:16).

Persis: 'my dear friend . . . another woman who's worked very hard in the Lord' (Romans 16:12).

Timothy: 'my true son in the faith' (1 Timothy 1:2); 'I have no one else like him' (Philippians 2:20); 'as a son with his father he has served with me in the work of the gospel' (Philippians 2:22).

Tychicus: 'a dear brother, a faithful minister and fellow servant in the Lord' (Colossians 4:7).

> *I'm convinced that one of the best ways to pursue biblical intimacy is to serve alongside brothers and sisters in gospel work.*

I'm convinced that one of the best ways to pursue biblical intimacy is to serve alongside brothers and sisters in gospel work. If we use our God-given gifts together to fulfil a shared vision, this can lead very naturally to a growing love both for the Lord Jesus and for our brothers and sisters in Christ.

More than a brush with royalty: David and Jonathan

David has just defeated the nation's biggest enemy and won a famous victory. This humble shepherd boy is now on an inevitable journey to become king of Israel. God's hand is on him. There are some telling reactions to David's rise to prominence, recorded in 1 Samuel 18:

The women of Israel *idolize* David:

> As they danced, they sang:
>   'Saul has slain his thousands,
>   and David his tens of thousands.'
> (verse 7)

Saul, the current king, is *envious* of David:

> Saul was very angry; this refrain displeased him greatly.
> 'They have credited David with tens of thousands,' he
> thought, 'but me with only thousands. What more can
> he get but the kingdom?' And from that time on Saul
> kept a close eye on David.
> (verses 8–9)

Jonathan *loves* David: 'Jonathan became one in spirit with David, and he loved him as himself' (verse 1).

Jonathan is King Saul's son and therefore heir to the throne. But unlike his father, he doesn't envy David. Neither does he idolize him with grand, overstated songs. No, Jonathan loves him. And to express that love, he does everything possible to encourage him as God's plan for his life unfolds. His humble acceptance of David as God's chosen king is symbolized when 'Jonathan took off the robe he was wearing and gave it to David, along with his tunic, and even his sword, his bow and his belt' (verse 4).

Now, as a same-sex attracted Christian, it's tempting to look at the description of David and Jonathan's friendship and apply it directly to me (and not only because one of them is my namesake). The idea of being 'one in spirit' with a Christian friend really appeals to me. And I long for the kind of godly, intimate love that these two men of faith shared together.

But before we rush to draw out principles for Christian intimacy, we need to remember (as Jesus teaches in Luke 24:27) that the Old Testament Scriptures point us to Christ and speak concerning him. David, soon to be Israel's king, is a forerunner of Jesus the King of kings. So Jonathan's love for, and delight in, David should first encourage Christians to love and delight in Christ.

With that caveat in mind, however, there are still things we can learn about human intimacy from the godly friendship between these two believing men.

I wonder, for example, how do we react when there's someone new on the scene? At church perhaps, or at work, or maybe just a new friend. We might be in awe of their skills, looks, ability or reputation, and make the same mistake as the women of Israel by idolizing them. Or we could react like Saul and be envious rather than thank God for the abilities he's entrusted to that person. The human heart can often swing from idolatry to envy. One way to help avoid sinful reactions is to ask: 'How might God be working in this person's life?' and 'How can I get alongside and encourage them, as God works out his purposes in and through them?'

As for Jonathan, he loyally sticks with his friend, even though his father sets out to pursue and kill David. In the heat of Saul's pursuit, we're given a beautiful snapshot of authentic biblical friendship: 'And Saul's son Jonathan went to David at Horesh and helped him to find strength in God' (1 Samuel 23:16).

Wouldn't that be a great goal to pursue as we seek to build intimate friendships with Christian brothers and sisters? Not to encourage them to become overly dependent on me, nor to put too much hope in them. But instead, to help one another find strength and encouragement in our relationship with God.

Radical allegiance: Ruth and Naomi

Naomi is a widow in a foreign land whose husband and two sons die. She pleads with her daughters-in-law, Ruth and Orpah, to leave her and return home. She has nothing to offer them – no more sons whom they could remarry, as was the custom in Israel (Deuteronomy 25:5–10).

We see two distinct reactions: 'Orpah kissed her mother-in-law goodbye', whereas Ruth 'clung to her' (Ruth 1:14). The verb (*dābaq*), describing Ruth's clinging to Naomi, is the same one used to describe commitment in marriage: a man shall 'hold fast to' his wife (Genesis 2:24 ESV). Ruth then makes a solemn commitment to Naomi:

> Where you go I will go, and where you lodge I will lodge.
> Your people shall be my people, and your God my God.
> Where you die I will die, and there will I be buried. May
> the LORD do so to me and more also if anything but death
> parts me from you.
> (Ruth 1:16–17 ESV)

Ruth leaves her family and homeland, never to return. She commits herself to a destitute widow, probably believing that she'll remain childless. Her commitment to Naomi is even more radical than marriage, which is binding only while the spouse lives. In contrast, Ruth is saying that she will die and be buried where Naomi dies. She promises her loyalty even beyond the grave.

And God uses Ruth's devotion to Naomi for his own glory. As the story unfolds, we learn that eventually she does marry and has a son. A son who, unknown to her, will be an ancestor of King David, from whose line comes Jesus the Son of God (Matthew 1:5–6).

In our sex-obsessed culture, it's easy to fall into the trap of believing that if we're not in a sexual relationship, we can't experience love or commitment. The book of Ruth explodes this myth. In a society where most people tend to look out for their own interests, believers can offer a powerful witness by showing this kind of sacrificial allegiance. To a family member perhaps, or to a brother or sister in Christ. And who knows how God, in his providence, may choose to work through such selfless dedication.

When I was suffering with depression and anxiety, two of my married friends demonstrated this type of radical allegiance in a very practical way. They assured me that if I were to end up homeless and still unable to work, I could move into their house for as long as necessary. They even offered to convert their loft so that I could have a private space. Well, they may have had in mind to preserve their own space, but I took it more positively! Either way, they displayed sacrificial love.

Expressions of affection or exclusion zone?

One of the best inventions of 2006, according to *Time* magazine, was a shirt that sends virtual hugs.[2] After the wearer cuddles themselves, the sensor shirt transmits the data to the other person's hug shirt via an app – so, body warmth, heartbeat and strength of touch. Their shirt then heats up and tingles to give them a virtual hug. No, I'm not making it up. You can buy one online – while stocks last.

How many people in our churches are crying out for affection today?

Behind this peculiar concept is a genuine desire for physical closeness. After I'd given a talk on intimacy once at a church conference, an elderly lady approached me. It was Joan's eighty-fifth birthday, but she'd kept it quiet as she didn't like to create a fuss. She had no family, and told me she hadn't been hugged in years. In an embarrassed whisper she asked, 'Could I have a birthday hug?' I was touched by this sweetest of requests. But I could have wept too. How many people in our churches are crying out for affection today?

I'm often asked if it's wrong for same-sex attracted Christians to enjoy intimacy that includes physical touch. We saw earlier that we must flee sexual immorality. So does this mean coning off a three-metre exclusion zone around all my same-sex friends, to ensure that nothing inappropriate takes place? Maybe I should make it four metres, just to be safe!

Well, there are certainly situations or times when an exclusion zone might be needed. For example, in the face of persistent temptations from Potiphar's wife, Joseph 'refused to go to bed with her or *even to be with her*' (Genesis 39:10, italics mine).

But pastorally, I always avoid laying down rules where God's word doesn't. The Bible gives us principles about how we should treat others, and God wants us to apply them wisely with the help of the Holy Spirit. So Timothy, for example, is instructed to 'treat younger men as brothers, older women as mothers, and younger women as sisters, with absolute purity' (1 Timothy 5:1–2). Notice that Timothy gets a godly principle to apply wisely, not a detailed rulebook to follow slavishly.

In considering what level of physical intimacy, if any, may be appropriate in a particular friendship, we must be driven by a desire to please and honour God. If my heart is not set on obeying God, then I'll inevitably struggle to pursue godly intimacy (whether physical or emotional) with other people.

Appropriate levels of physical touch will vary for each one of us. So what might be innocent affection for one person could prove to be a temptation for another. I'm naturally a very tactile person, whereas I have friends who shy away at the prospect of a bear hug! And I always respect this, so they don't need to run when they see me approaching. That said,

I'm convinced that many of our fears and discomforts concerning physical affection tend to be culturally conditioned, rather than driven by clear biblical thinking.

There is no indication that Jesus was concerned about outward expressions of affection from one of his closest friends. At the Last Supper he has just predicted his betrayal and is troubled in spirit. At that moment there's a beautiful description of his physical closeness to John. Sadly, most modern translations don't reflect this, but the King James Version captures the more literal meaning of the Greek: 'Now there was leaning on Jesus' bosom one of his disciples, whom Jesus loved . . . He then lying on Jesus' breast saith unto him, Lord, who is it? (John 13:23, 25 KJV).

John, the disciple whom Jesus loved, was physically close to his Lord. He was resting on Jesus' bosom/breast, perhaps able to hear the very heartbeat of God. Can you imagine two Christian brothers doing that today during a bring-and-share lunch at your church? How would people react?

From a personal perspective, I've learnt that if I'm starved of all physical touch, then I'm much more likely to crave intimacy in all the wrong places. Yes, of course we must avoid sexual immorality, and yes, we must absolutely pray for pure hearts. But I'm convinced that the Lord Jesus does not command his unmarried followers to live lives that are devoid of any physical affection.

Shocking eulogy – for the other Jonathan

Imagine the following brief conversation between a husband and wife at bedtime, just before they go off to sleep. Or if you're married, perhaps you can try to imagine having this conversation with your spouse:

'Darling, I forgot to mention that I've made a new friend at church.'

'Oh, that's nice dear.'

'Yes, and their love for me is wonderful, more wonderful even than the erotic love that you and I enjoy together. Good night.' *(Switches light off)*

Admittedly, an unlikely conversation. But it highlights the shock value of this extract from David's lament after he hears that both Saul and Jonathan are dead:

> I grieve for you, Jonathan my brother;
>> you were very dear to me.
> Your love for me was wonderful,
>> more wonderful than that of women.
> (2 Samuel 1:26)

Now remember, this is David. He knew quite a lot about the love of women. But he recognizes that the self-giving, God-exalting, covenant-keeping, brotherly love of his friend Jonathan was 'more wonderful' even than the erotic love he'd experienced with women.

As an unmarried man, I find this a hugely encouraging reminder that sexual intimacy is not essential to life. But more than that, I'm excited by the possibility of continuing to discover and enjoy a 'more wonderful' love with my brothers and sisters in Christ.

Whether we're married or not, in seeking to enjoy intimacy with others, we're to delight in Christ as our first love and look to him to satisfy our deepest longings. And springing from that essential union, we should also take delight in Christian brothers and sisters. David seemed to have the balance right when he wrote:

I say to the LORD, 'You are my Lord;
    apart from you I have no good thing.'
I say of the holy people who are in the land,
    'They are the noble ones in whom is all my delight.'
    (Psalm 16:2–3)

12. THE GIFT OF BEING UNMARRIED

I will betroth you to me for ever;
I will betroth you in righteousness and justice,
in love and compassion.
(Hosea 2:19)

You could be next: Rob's story

The weekend was going to be special. One of those rare occasions when my family would all be together – Mum, Dad, two brothers, my sister-in-law and niece. Rick's photo rests proudly on my parents' mantelpiece, as he is a close family friend. And now he was getting married.

Here are a few of the things various people said to me during the day:

'So have you found anyone yet?' to which I thought, 'Actually I'm not even looking.'

'Don't worry, I'm sure there's someone out there for you,' to which I thought, 'Wow, thanks for the huge self-esteem boost.'

'Just think, Rob. You could be next,' to which I thought, 'I bet you wouldn't dare say that at a funeral.'

I always approach weddings positively. But as hard as I try to fight the negative thoughts, I usually end up feeling depressed. And this time was no different. Maybe it was all the talk of marriage, relationships, love and family, or perhaps it was all the children running around. It just seemed to drive home the feeling that I'm the only single person left and I'm missing out. That somehow I'm just not 'normal'.

No rush to marry

Marriage is in decline. Back in 1972 around 7.8% of the male population and 6.1% of the female population in the UK got married. But how things have changed! By 2009 the annual figure had dropped to 2.1% and 1.9% respectively.[1] And at the last count approximately 7.1 million of us were living alone.[2] People today seem to be in no rush to get married.

Church leaders have long lamented this decline in marriage and the associated detrimental effects on society and children. And it's right, of course, that Christians defend and confidently proclaim biblical marriage as God's good design and as the God-ordained environment in which to bring up children. But there is a danger. By upholding and affirming a high view of marriage, we can inadvertently downgrade the immense value and importance of unmarried life.

A notable theme tune runs right throughout the one chapter in the Bible that deals extensively with both marriage and singleness. And it may come as a surprise to you. Why not follow the thread through for yourself, looking up each of these phrases in 1 Corinthians 7 within their immediate context?

'Stay unmarried, as I do' (verse 8).
'She must remain unmarried or else be reconciled to her husband' (verse 11).

'She must not divorce him' (verse 13).
'Each person should live . . . in whatever situation
the Lord has assigned to them' (verse 17).
'Each person should remain in the situation they
were in when God called them' (verse 20).
'Each person, as responsible to God, should remain
in the situation they were in' (verse 24).
'I think that it is good for a man to remain as he is'
(verse 26).
'She is happier if she stays as she is' (verse 40).

Now if you've looked up those partial verses, you'll know that
Paul isn't addressing the specific issue of marriage and singleness in every single one. But we're interested in the dominant
note of the chapter. And that, I think, is very clear. Paul is
urging the Corinthians, as a general rule, to remain as they
are. To be in no rush to move on from the situation they were
in when God saved them.

Two highly valued gifts

'So do you have a wife and family, Jonathan?'

Someone I'd not met before at church asked me this
question. I used to reply to such enquiries by saying that no,
I'm single. But I'd been mulling over a different response,
mainly in the hope of avoiding the thinly veiled looks of
pity. And it was time to give my newly fashioned answer its
debut:

'No, I have the gift of being unmarried.'

Awkward silence for a brief moment. Nothing new there.
But I detected no look of pity. Instead, I saw intrigue written
on the enquirer's face. After a pause, she pressed me. Why use
that phrase, rather than say I'm single? It led to the most

stimulating, encouraging conversation I've ever had about my marital status.

Now you may feel this is pure semantics. After all, one of the dictionary definitions of the adjective 'single' is 'unmarried or not in a romantic relationship'. But to my ears (and it seems to the ears of those who look at me with pity), 'single' feels loaded with negativity. The word can assume a life of its own and carry with it the meaning of aloneness, sadness and isolation. By contrast, 'unmarried' sounds more like an objective fact, a status.

> *Two gifts. Each one from God, and each, therefore, is to be highly valued and definitely not despised.*

Whichever word we prefer, Paul, an unmarried man, writes to the Corinthian Christians: 'I wish that all of you were as I am. But each of you has your own gift from God; one has this gift, another has that' (1 Corinthians 7:7).

Two gifts. Each one from God, and each, therefore, is to be highly valued and definitely not despised. The Greek word is *charisma*, literally 'a gift of grace, an undeserved favour'. Paul uses the same word in Romans 12:6 to refer to the 'different gifts' that we have 'according to the grace given to each of us'.

But what if I don't have the gift of being unmarried?

This question crops up a lot when I teach on this subject. Some people simply don't feel 'called' to the single life, or are convinced God hasn't given them this gift. Others I know do have a strong sense of calling, and have chosen to remain unmarried for the sake of the gospel.

But I don't think Paul teaches us to think about singleness and marriage as subjective spiritual callings. He simply says in 1 Corinthians 7 that, as an objective reality, each has their own gift of grace from God. So if you're married right now, that's your gift. If you're unmarried right now, then that's your gift. And in each situation God's grace will sustain you. But that's not to say that an unmarried person shouldn't pray for, or even eagerly desire, the other gift.

We also need to remember that virtually everyone who right now has the gift of marriage will, at some point in the future, have the gift of being unmarried. Except, of course, in the unlikely event that you and your spouse pass away at the exact same moment. Similarly, some of those who right now have the gift of singleness will at some point receive the gift of being married. So neither marriage nor singleness are necessarily to be seen as permanent gifts.

Choosing what's better

So being married and unmarried are both gifts. But which is better? There seems to be a rush towards the marriage department in our churches, whereas the singleness section of the store doesn't seem quite as desirable. But how do single Christians know if they should be pursuing marriage? Sadly, many unmarried Christians aren't even encouraged to ask this question. In many churches the assumption is that everyone should be working towards marriage.

While teaching at a Bible college, I was told of one large evangelical church where, in the middle of a Sunday service, the pastor asked all the adults under twenty-five to stand up. He then told those who were already married to sit down again. 'Now look around,' he said to those still standing. 'There's no reason why you shouldn't be married. What are you waiting for?'

Isn't that tragic? It's vital that every local church learns to value single people and communicate a positive view of the unmarried life. I would encourage any church leaders reading this book to ensure that whenever you teach about marriage, you also teach a high view of singleness. Look how positive Paul is. So positive that he encourages Christians in Corinth to remain unmarried: 'I wish that all of you were as I am . . . Now to the unmarried and the widows I say: it is good for them to stay unmarried, as I do' (1 Corinthians 7:7–8).

Now Paul may have in mind here what he later calls the 'present crisis' (verse 26). This could have been specific to Corinth, or he may be thinking more generally of the urgency of gospel work and the ability of unmarried people to stay fully devoted to God.

Whatever Paul's reasons, he goes on to teach that being unmarried has some real advantages. But he doesn't restrict us. So it's certainly not wrong to search for a spouse: 'If you do marry, you have not sinned; and if a virgin marries, she has not sinned' (1 Corinthians 7:28). Indeed, far from being wrong, 'He who finds a wife finds what is good and receives favour from the LORD' (Proverbs 18:22).

So, if you're a Christian who struggles with same-sex temptations, it's not wrong for you to desire biblical marriage. You can pray for it and actively seek it. But we need to ensure that we don't put our hope in finding a spouse, or let our happiness rest on our marital status. And if we're ever tempted to see marriage as the solution to all our woes, well, Paul provides a sharp wake-up call: 'Those who marry will face many troubles in this life, and I want to spare you this' (1 Corinthians 7:28).

Rob eventually snapped out of his dejection at Rick's wedding by recognizing that he'd allowed his desires to shrivel up and to focus on the small, temporary joys and pleasures of this world. And then by focusing on what Paul calls the 'better' gift of not being married, Rob reminded himself of the unparalleled joy that Jesus promises to those who believe in him. True, neither Rob nor I have a wife. But we do have someone much more desirable, one who will never let us down:

> Whom have I in heaven but you?
>   And earth has nothing I desire besides you.
> My flesh and my heart may fail,
>   but God is the strength of my heart
>   and my portion for ever.
> (Psalm 73:25–26)

Free from daily concern?

Rob and I were both exhausted after a long day of Bible teaching and pastoral appointments at Capernwray Bible School. We now had a five-hour drive ahead of us. Actually, make that seven hours – 'M6, J14–18, Severe delays,' warned the motorway sign above.

'Could we do this if we each had a wife and kids?' Rob pondered.

It was a fascinating question. Away from our homes for several days at a time. Early mornings, late nights. Shut away for hours on end preparing teaching material. Post-preaching blues, and that frequent desire just to crash and do nothing when you finally get home.

'I don't know how married people cope,' I replied. 'Just imagine if I had to call my wife now: "Darling, I'm not going to be home until 2 am – please kiss Daniel, Isaiah, Hannah and Phoebe good night."'

There are, of course, many married people who do manage to serve God with passionate devotion. And they have my utmost respect and admiration. Personally, though, I've come to recognize and celebrate the tremendous privilege and freedom that I have to serve the Lord as an unmarried man. As Paul writes,

> I would like you to be free from concern. An unmarried man is concerned about the Lord's affairs – how he can please the Lord. But a married man is concerned about the affairs of this world – how he can please his wife – and his interests are divided. An unmarried woman or virgin is concerned about the Lord's affairs: her aim is to be devoted to the Lord in both body and spirit. But a married woman is concerned about the affairs of this world – how she can please her husband. I am saying this for your own good, not to restrict you, but that you may live in a right way in undivided devotion to the Lord.
> (1 Corinthians 7:32–35)

However, please let's note that being unmarried is only a gift if I use the freedom this brings in the right way. Being free from concern about how to please a spouse is not intended as a licence to please myself. The single life can all too easily become the selfish life. So I'm sometimes guilty of celebrating singleness for the wrong reasons: the joy of not having to fight over the TV remote, for example, or just enjoying my own space a little bit too much. However, devotion to myself is not the gift that Paul has in mind. No, the biblical gift of being unmarried is the ability to serve the Lord Jesus, the King of the universe, with 'undivided devotion'.

If you or someone you're supporting is currently single but considering marriage, it's worth perhaps pausing, reflecting, praying and asking the following questions: will marriage help me to be fully devoted to God or will remaining unmarried, with my devotions and interests undivided, allow me to better glorify God and serve him more effectively?

But what if I burn with passion?

Jeremy had been invited to church by his friend. He was in his mid-sixties and planning to convert his civil partnership into a same-sex marriage. He politely introduced himself to me after I'd preached from 1 Corinthians 7.

'You missed out verse 9: "But if they cannot control themselves, they should marry, for it is better to marry than to burn with passion."' He continued, 'That means it's acceptable for someone to be a Christian and have a gay marriage, doesn't it?'

It wasn't the first time I'd been asked this type of question. Here's what I said:

- We must allow scripture to interpret scripture.

As we saw earlier, Paul has already clearly stated in 1 Corinthians 6 that same-sex practice is sinful. So his solution for same-sex temptations cannot involve entering into a same-sex relationship.

- We mustn't read our cultural assumptions back into the text.

When Paul uses the term 'marry', he's obviously referring to biblical, heterosexual marriage, as defined by God in Genesis 2:24 and reinforced by Jesus.

- Marriage is not the only route to dousing the flames of passion.

Marriage is not the complete, or the only, solution for sexual temptation. Many married friends of mine tell me that they still struggle with lust. And elsewhere Paul says that each of us – married or unmarried – has an obligation, by the Spirit, to 'put to death the misdeeds of the body' (Romans 8:13).

Unwrapping the gift

Picture a six-year-old boy and a nine-year-old girl sitting under the Christmas tree, shivering with wintry excitement. Wrapping paper and labels everywhere. Every single present has been opened. Smiles abound. A typical Christmas morning scene, you might think.

At times, I've wanted to go back to God and ask if he'd kept the receipt.

But the two faces also betray a trace of guilty pleasure and apprehension. The time is 4 am. And did I mention that all the presents have been opened? Yes, I meant every single one, whoever the intended recipient. My sister and I had fervently unwrapped the lot. And now – somewhat less enthusiastically – we were waiting for Mum and Dad to wake up.

Looking back on my Christian life, I haven't always had a childlike eagerness to unwrap the gift of being unmarried. At times, like many of my unmarried friends, I've wanted to go back to God and ask if he'd kept the receipt.

But one of the many good things the Lord cultivated in my heart as he brought me through my anxiety and depression was a determination to embrace and celebrate this gift. It's been a process. And it's still ongoing. I'm still learning to explore and enjoy the benefits of being devoted to 'the Lord's affairs', and I frequently fail to 'live in a right way in undivided devotion'. There are still days when I yearn for the wrong kind of intimacy and am tempted to wallow in self-pity.

In the interests of remaining upbeat, though, here are five convictions that have helped me move from reluctant recipient to grateful beneficiary.

Becoming a grateful beneficiary

1. *Singleness should not equate to sadness, loneliness and frustration*

As we saw earlier, Jesus promises abundant life. True, we won't enjoy complete abundance this side of heaven: 'Now I know in part; then I shall know fully, even as I am fully known' (1 Corinthians 13:12). The unmarried person may well experience times of dejection. But we can also expect foretastes of the promised fullness. And if we're willing to embrace the gift, the unmarried life can indeed be a genuinely fulfilling, joyful life.

2. *Relating to Jesus is not burdensome*

I learnt many things in my ten years as an unmarried church pastor. Not least that it's not always easy for Christians to keep their spouse happy. So I often thank God that I'm free to focus all my energy on pleasing the one who says, 'My yoke is easy and my burden is light' (Matthew 11:30).

Sure, obeying Jesus can be demanding. But knowing what he expects of me is straightforward. I'm reliably informed by some of my married friends that it's not always so easy to know what their spouse expects of them! In fact, what spouses expect from one another can fluctuate from day to day, according to how they feel. Not so with Jesus. He is the same yesterday, today and forever.

3. *Jesus more than makes up for what we give up*

Let's be honest. Many of us who are same-sex attracted don't find it easy to say no to a same-sex relationship. But if we give up anything, or anyone, for the sake of following Jesus, we won't be short-changed. Jesus is no man's debtor. 'Truly I tell you . . . no one who has left home or wife or brothers or sisters or parents or children for the sake of the kingdom of God will fail to receive many times as much in this age, and in the age to come eternal life' (Luke 18:29–30).

4. Hospitality begins at home

Some single friends complain that people at church never invite them around for meals. A while ago I resolved not to complain, but to act. Now, I'm not a great cook. Come to my home and you'll probably be offered takeaway pizza or a Mr Kipling cake, not a gourmet three-course meal. But by God's grace I can still warmly welcome you and hopefully make you feel at home. Isn't that the core of true hospitality?

5. There is no greater joy than unbridled devotion to the Lord

I know this is true. I passionately believe it. My most joyful moments have been when I've delighted in loving and serving the Lord Jesus. But I have much to learn. Far too often I have foolishly set my heart on other things or on other people – then wondered why my joy fades. Verses like the following inspire me, though, to keep pursuing satisfaction in Christ:

My soul will be satisfied as with fat and rich food,
    and my mouth will praise you with joyful lips,
when I remember you upon my bed,
    and meditate on you in the watches of the night;
for you have been my help,
    and in the shadow of your wings I will sing for joy.
(Psalm 63:5–7 ESV)

13. THE FUTURE OF MARRIAGE

May your fountain be blessed,
and may you rejoice in the wife of your youth.
(Proverbs 5:18)

Diving in

'How can someone be so romantically stupid?' exclaimed Hayley in frustration.

Wearing her wedding dress, she sat in the spartan, moist, tiled, swimming pool changing room. She was worried that she might not be able to go through with it, in light of the venue her fiancé had picked out.

I was watching *Don't Tell the Bride* while waiting for my friend Ethan to arrive. Actually, 'watching' would be to overstate it. I made the mistake of channel-hopping for a few minutes, and landed on this so-called reality TV programme where couples are given £14,000 for their dream wedding. Too good to be true? Well, the twist is that the groom has to organize the event and decide on every little detail. The bride is left completely in the dark. Choosing a swimming pool as the wedding venue is probably the strangest decision yet. A close second is the groom who decided to send his bride to a theme park for a pre-wedding roller-coaster ride.

Like the brides in the programme, many people have preconceived notions about what constitutes the perfect, romantic wedding. But with so much focus on planning the big day, sadly the essential investment of time, energy and commitment to prepare for the marriage itself often gets squeezed out.

Christians too can get drawn into an overly romanticized view of marriage. The search for a prospective spouse can sometimes end up focusing almost entirely on mutual attraction and the quest for that intangible spark. This over-emphasis on romance, sexual attraction and feelings means that those who battle with same-sex temptations often feel automatically excluded from even the possibility of hetero-sexual marriage.

Tough act to follow

'I face all the same challenges as other married people,' explained Ethan. 'My same-sex temptations are just one issue that Liz and I are working through together. And it's not even close to being the main area of struggle for me. To be honest, having a joint bank account has been a far greater challenge.'

My hospitality enablers, Domino's, had just delivered dinner, saving my culinary blushes. Ethan and I were having a first proper catch-up since his wedding day just over a year ago. I was interested to know how things were going, and how I could be praying for him and his wife. And in particular, I wondered how he was coping with his ongoing same-sex desires.

But I had an ulterior motive too. I was in the process of writing this book and wanted to include a chapter on marriage.

I always tread especially carefully when I write on subjects about which I have no personal experience. Well, I have personal experience of observing and relating to married couples – and it's surprising how much you can learn about the joy (or otherwise) of marriage as a dispassionate outsider. But it isn't the same. So I wanted Ethan's wise, godly input and advice.

Ethan is twenty-nine years old and has struggled with same-sex desires since childhood. He'd always longed to have a wife and family, though, so I was delighted when he announced his engagement. He was somewhat concerned at the time, as he felt little sexual attraction towards Liz. But he rightly recognized that the more important question was whether he was willing to commit himself to this incredibly demanding calling: 'Husbands, love your wives, just as Christ loved the church and gave himself up for her' (Ephesians 5:25).

'Liz always understood that the physical side of the relationship might be really difficult for me. And she was more than willing to accept that my sexual desires for her might not grow significantly. Her big concern was whether or not I was ready to be fully committed to her, and to model my love for her on Christ's love for his church. And I was. Sure, it's a really tough calling. But I love sharing my life with her and serving Christ alongside her.'

As we chatted, I realized that the kinds of struggles Ethan and Liz face are not really unique. Yes, he still battles with same-sex desires and has to resist temptation. But all of his married friends still battle with opposite-sex desires, and they too have to resist temptation. The key question is whether or not he's determined to remain faithful to Liz, to keep praying for the grace to love her as Christ loves the church. And he clearly is. He exuded a passionate commitment.

So how does Christ love the church?

In a word: sacrificially. Jesus 'gave himself up for her'. In his earthly ministry he set out to serve rather than to be served, to wash the feet of his disciples, to put the needs of others before his own. And such was his great love for the church that he was willing to hand himself over to a cruel, barbaric, humiliating death for her sake. Jesus, the Son of God, put his bride, the church, first.

When I was a pastor, couples who were having difficulties in their marriage would sometimes approach me (yes, me, an unmarried man!) for advice. On occasions the problems were so complex and deep-rooted that I'd have no option but to refer them – much to my relief – to one of the married elders, or sometimes for professional marriage counselling.

But often it wasn't too difficult for me, as an outsider, to spot the essential problem. And one of the most frequent root causes was selfishness. One or other of the couple putting themselves first, or insisting on their rights, or not listening to their spouse's point of view and not taking their needs, feelings or desires into consideration. In other words, not loving with Christlike, giving-yourself-up, other-person-centred love.

Even in marriages where one person struggles with same-sex temptations, I've found that, more often than not, sex is not the key issue that causes friction. As one friend said, 'The 99% of my married life when we're not having sex is where I need to focus the majority of my time and efforts if the marriage is to flourish.'

Pastor and author Tim Keller has wise advice for married people:

We must say to ourselves something like this: 'Well, when Jesus looked down from the cross, he didn't think "I am giving myself to you because you are so attractive to me." No, he was in agony, and he looked down at us – denying him, abandoning him, and betraying him – and in the greatest act of love in history, he STAYED. He said, "Father, forgive them, they don't know what they are doing." He loved us, not because we were lovely to him, but to make us lovely. That is why I am going to love my spouse.' Speak to your heart like that, and then fulfil the promises you made on your wedding day.[1]

Close encounter

I met Monica at a coffee bar outreach for international students. She was from Switzerland (what is it with me and Swiss people?) and visiting the UK to improve her English. She was passionate about her faith, and we immediately hit if off. There was a definite spark of . . . well, something I hadn't quite felt before.

Did I find her attractive? Most definitely. She was physically beautiful, and I could see that. Was I attracted to her? Well, yes, but not in a sexual way. What I found most appealing was that she really loved Jesus. She possessed the one thing that I always told myself would be absolutely crucial if I were ever to get married. The apostle Peter describes it much better than I can:

> Your beauty should not come from outward adornment, such as elaborate hairstyles and the wearing of gold jewellery or fine clothes. Rather, it should be that of your inner self, the unfading beauty of a gentle and quiet spirit, which is of great worth in God's sight.
>
> (1 Peter 3:3–4)

Now 'quiet', Monica certainly is not. She has a strong, vivacious personality and knows how to enjoy life to the full. But she does have a 'gentle and quiet spirit', and it was this unfading beauty that ultimately drew me to her. We became great friends, and we loved to chat and walk and pray and read the Bible and sing together. I was honest with her about my background and ongoing struggle with same-sex desires. She responded with love, grace and acceptance.

When she returned home we stayed in touch by writing regular letters (for the uninitiated, letter-writing is an ancient form of communication using tools known as 'pens' and 'paper'). I also visited her in Switzerland, and she made return visits to the UK. I hoped and prayed that in time something more might develop, that perhaps marriage could even be on the horizon.

In the end my lack of sexual attraction wasn't the deal-breaker, although this did, of course, concern me. But my greater worry was that I wouldn't be able to commit myself to love and care for Monica, not with that same passion and commitment with which I'd loved Jean-Luc in my life before Christ. The calling to love her as Christ loves the church was, sadly, one that I just did not believe I could live up to.

Monica and I have been great friends for over twenty years now. She's married to Daniel, and I count both of them among my very closest friends. The three of us regularly go on holiday together, and we always enjoy rich fellowship in Christ and laugh a lot. Indeed, part of this book was written during one such holiday in south Wales. Only the providential God of all grace, with his smiling face, could have planned that outcome!

Thinking of getting married?

Some of you might be actively exploring the possibility of marriage. Or might possibly be in the process of planning a wedding and preparing for marriage, but concerned about how a same-sex struggle may impact on it. Each person is unique, of course, and each will struggle in their own individual ways, according to background, life experiences, temperament, personality and so on. Therefore what follows can only be very general in nature.

The Church of England states that marriage 'must not be undertaken carelessly, lightly, or selfishly, but reverently, responsibly, and after serious thought'.[2] With this in mind, I'd strongly urge you and your prospective spouse to seek pastoral advice from a church leader, or from spiritually mature and trusted friends. Obviously, the consequences of someone who struggles with same-sex attractions rushing into heterosexual marriage can be devastating and far-reaching, and can negatively impact many lives.

You might also both find it helpful to contact True Freedom Trust.[3] We're often able to put couples in touch with others who've got married in similar circumstances. For many people, marriage has proved to be a great blessing.

Here are some areas to consider prayerfully and talk through. These are based on the experiences of various people with same-sex temptations who are now married to someone of the opposite sex.

Be passionate about a Christ-centred marriage

Think about whether the person you're considering as a marriage partner will help you to love and serve the Lord Jesus. Pray together. Read the Bible together. Talk about your faith together. Worship God together. If he isn't the primary focus when you're getting to know someone, you'll likely struggle to build a Christ-centred marriage. Will you be able to serve together, and will your different gifts and areas of service complement each other?

Be prepared for the whole of married life

Most married couples (I'm reliably informed) don't spend most of their time having sex. So it's important to consider how you'll cope with the many other aspects of married life. Read some good Christian books on marriage together.[4] Attend preparation classes at your church if they're offered. If not, then consider asking a spiritually mature, godly Christian couple to help you prepare. They may also be willing to provide ongoing support and advice in the early months of marriage.

Be honest with any potential spouse

Honesty and trust are the bedrock of any good relationship, and vital ingredients of a stable marriage. It's important to be candid with any potential marriage partner about your same-sex attractions. This probably won't be an easy conversation. But the sooner you bite the bullet, the more time you will have to work through the issues and to determine if marriage is viable.

Be careful not to focus too much on attraction

You don't need to find every person of the opposite sex in the world attractive – if you think about it, it's much better if you don't! But what you do need is to find one Christian whom you can love and commit yourself to, forsaking all others (men and women). Pray for God's wisdom and leading in this.

Yes, it's important that you find that person attractive, as you're committing to share the rest of your life with him or her. But sexual attraction is not the only element needed. Do you find their character, personality and gifting attractive? Are you drawn to them because they love Jesus and pursue godliness? After all, these things will last, whereas physical beauty is likely only to fade over time.

Be sure of your true identity

Remember, as we saw in chapter 7, your true identity is in Christ rather than in your sexual attractions. Yes, your struggle will impact the marriage to one degree or another. But it is possible to make too much of it, and for it to become the defining issue, to the exclusion of other areas that you'll need to focus on and work through together.

Be sensitive to a potential spouse's needs

Your same-sex attractions will affect your partner too, especially if they're insecure about their looks and desirability. Some people are better equipped than others to take on the 'challenge' of marrying someone with this struggle. If your partner is likely to need constant reassurance that you find him or her the most attractive person in the world, could this put you and the marriage under too much strain?

Be honest with yourself about sex

Sex is a good gift from God and, as the Song of Songs shows, is intended to be an enjoyable and celebrated aspect of married life. That said, it is by no means the most important aspect. But Paul does teach that sexual intercourse is a marital duty (1 Corinthians 7:2–5), rather than just a bit of fun when both people are 'in the mood'. This is also an area where Christlike, self-giving love needs to be expressed, with each partner being more concerned about how to please their spouse than how to please themselves.

So think about how you'd both cope if one of you wanted sex more than the other. Or imagine if you weren't able to get aroused or didn't find sex enjoyable. How might this affect the relationship or your (and your spouse's) confidence?

Be ready for difficulties

Every marriage goes through rocky times. And yours would be no different. Marriage brings together two people with a sinful nature, both of whom carry their own emotional baggage. You might be managing your same-sex temptations, but is your prospective spouse dealing with their own personal struggles?

Even if same-sex desires are generally under control, they can often resurface with a vengeance when things get tough. It's important to have a coping strategy in place if this happens. Will you be able to talk to your spouse, or to a close Christian friend? In a culture that will urge you to 'be true to yourself' and find a same-sex partner, will you remain true to Christ and faithful to your spouse?

Be realistic, not idealistic, about marriage

It probably doesn't need saying at this point, but don't approach marriage as if it will resolve your same-sex attractions, or act as a magic-bullet solution to loneliness, insecurities or low self-esteem. The things that are brought into a marriage often come to the surface and are accentuated by married life, rather than being automatically fixed by it.

Also, make sure you are not just in love with the idea of marriage itself. And don't pursue marriage because of social, family or even church pressure. You must strongly desire to share your whole life with a spouse and resolve to love them 'till death us do part', with Christlike devotion.

Bride to be

Marriage can be an idol. Marriage can be neglected. Both are tragedies.

You may be reading this and fighting for your marriage. Or maybe you're not fighting but rejoicing, because you're really enjoying your married life. Others of you may be single and have a fervent desire to get married, or perhaps you're unmarried for the sake of the gospel. Whatever marriage might mean to you now, in the age to come it will be entirely different.

Jesus makes this surprising statement about the future of marriage when the Sadducees (who didn't believe in the resurrection) test him: 'You are in error because you do not know the Scriptures or the power of God. At the resurrection people will neither marry nor be given in marriage; they will be like the angels in heaven' (Matthew 22:29–30).

Marriage is temporary. It's not eternal. Knowing this should help us keep it in perspective, because there's a time coming when no-one will be married to another person. Reflect on this for a moment: at the time of the most overwhelming joy there will be no marriage. And at the time when we'll have more pleasure than we can ever imagine there will be no sex.

> *At the time when we'll have more pleasure than we can ever imagine there will be no sex.*

Marriage in this life foreshadows a single beautiful marriage that every Christian will be involved in. I'm often captivated by this heavenly vision:

> 'Let us rejoice and be glad
>   and give him glory!
> For the wedding of the Lamb has come,
>   and his bride has made herself ready.
> Fine linen, bright and clean,
>   was given her to wear.'
> (Fine linen stands for the righteous acts of God's holy people.)

> Then the angel said to me, 'Write this: Blessed are those who are invited to the wedding supper of the Lamb!' And he added, 'These are the true words of God.'
> (Revelation 19:7–9)

If you're a believer, single or married, you can look forward with great anticipation to the wedding feast of the Lamb, where Christ will be the bridegroom and the church will be his bride. This wedding supper will be the most satisfying one that any of us has ever enjoyed.

14. THE HOPE OF GLORY

God has chosen to make known among the Gentiles
the glorious riches of this mystery, which is
Christ in you, the hope of glory.
(Colossians 1:27)

Believing in the God of the impossible

'I don't want be to be gay,' nineteen-year-old Harry told me
bluntly. 'I'd love to have a wife and children in the future. Do
you believe God's able to intervene miraculously to change
my same-sex attractions? Can he make me straight?'

It wasn't that Harry's family and friends were giving him a
rough time over his sexuality. Nobody knew anyway. Everyone
assumed he hadn't found the right girl yet, or was preoccupied
with his studies. But since the age of thirteen he'd been pre-
dominately same-sex attracted. He struck me as a passionate
Christian who knew that God loved him deeply and accepted
him fully in Christ. Harry wasn't under any external pressure to
'change', either from his Christian parents or from his evangelical church. Yes, he believed that God's word forbids same-sex
practice, but he didn't even want a same-sex relationship. It
had never appealed to him. He longed to marry a woman.

I paused for a brief moment before responding, and prayed silently for wisdom. I've been asked this kind of question countless times before, but it never seems to get easier to answer. I wanted to give Harry hope. But true biblical hope, not empty false hope.

The way we usually use the word 'hope' today has more to do with wishful thinking or vague longing. So I hope that Arsenal might win the Premier League this year. But Rob tells me this is a vain hope (and, as much as I hate to admit it, he's probably right). You might hope for a great British summer, or that your minister doesn't preach for too long on a Sunday, or for any number of things that will probably prove in the end to be forlorn hopes.

Biblical hope is very different. It is rooted in the unbreakable promises of God in Scripture. Christians hope with sure and certain expectation, rather than with glass-half-full optimism. And biblical hope is mostly future hope too. So in the book of Hebrews the Holy Spirit speaks of believers being 'greatly encouraged' by 'the hope set before us', and declares that 'we have this hope as an anchor for the soul, firm and secure' (Hebrews 6:18–19).

'In answering a question about salvation,' I replied to Harry, 'Jesus spoke about the God *with whom all things are possible* [Matthew 19:26]. So with that aspect of God's nature in mind, I'd say that yes, God is certainly *able* to change your same-sex attractions. He is *able* to intervene miraculously, dramatically, even instantaneously. But perhaps the more important question is "will he do that?", or "should we expect that?"'

You might want to take a pill for that

'Over-realized eschatology' is one of my favourite terms. I smile whenever I read it or say it out loud. It sounds like something you should see your doctor about and ask him to prescribe a cream to rub into, or some pills to swallow. But it's a theological ailment rather than a physical one. Eschatology is the study of the end times, or of things to do with the end times. So if your eschatology is over-realized, it means that you're expecting God to do *in full* now what he's only promised to do *in full* in the future, in the age to come.

There are good reasons to believe this may have been a problem in first-century Ephesus. When Paul writes to Timothy, he urges this young(ish) pastor and teacher to 'command certain people not to teach false doctrines any longer' (1 Timothy 1:3). Then in his second letter he writes about 'Hymenaeus and Philetus, who have departed from the truth. They say that the resurrection has already taken place, and they destroy the faith of some' (2 Timothy 2:17–18).

Now if the Ephesians believed this false teaching that the general resurrection had already taken place, there would have been nothing more for them to look forward to. They would have expected to experience all of God's blessings now, in full. And they certainly wouldn't have expected to suffer, or to struggle.

But don't you just need to have faith?

In his desperation to be free from same-sex desires, young Harry had been undergoing therapy for the past few months. His therapist had categorically promised that God would give him complete freedom from same-sex temptations if he stayed the course.

However, to make promises such as this one is completely unbiblical, of course, and potentially very harmful to people who are often vulnerable. But sadly, I've met many others who, in the name of Christ, have been guaranteed similar outcomes. All they have to do, it is claimed, is to undergo a certain course of therapy, pursue a particular methodology, or attend a specific conference. Sometimes they just need to 'have faith' and 'believe'. But when these promised things don't happen, this can lead to a person's faith being shipwrecked.

I was stunned to learn of one method this professing Christian therapist had used in order to 'encourage' the process of change. He would show Harry pornographic pictures of women and, to stimulate arousal, ask him to imagine getting sexually intimate with them. As I listened, Jesus' warning came to mind that anyone who looks at a woman lustfully has already committed adultery with her in his heart (Matthew 5:28).

Harry, though, had been cooperating fully and doing everything asked of him, even those things with which he felt uncomfortable. He genuinely wanted to change, although so far nothing was working, and his same-sex desires seemed intractable.

Those who promise that a person's sexual attractions will change have an over-realized eschatology. There's certainly a time coming when every believer in Christ will be utterly free from every temptation, every ungodly desire and every effect of the fall. And God, in his mercy and grace, often gives us foretastes in this world of the fullness of life and freedom to come. But nowhere are we promised complete freedom from temptation and struggle in this life. Those who teach such things are claiming, in effect, that the resurrection has already taken place.

If you are the church leader, youth worker or friend of a same-sex attracted Christian, it is really important not to give an unbiblical guarantee that God will definitely set them free from same-sex temptations. The simple truth is that none of us knows for sure how God might choose to work in the life of a Christian struggling in this area.

So is there no place for counselling or therapy?

In contrast to a number of horror stories shared with me, I should stress that others have recounted how they have been greatly helped by wise, ethical counselling and therapy, rooted in biblical truth. Indeed, some friends (including Ethan, mentioned in the previous chapter) have, with the help of godly counselling, experienced a lessening of their same-sex desires, and a corresponding increase in opposite-sex desires. Some have gone on to enjoy a mutually fulfilling and stable heterosexual marriage. However, virtually all of the people I've met tell me that they still experience some measure of attraction to the same sex.

Sadly, there is a relentless drive today to deny people the right to voluntarily seek counselling and therapeutic help in ordering their sexual desires and behaviour according to their convictions of faith. This, it seems to me, goes against the principle of respecting client autonomy. The client's right to be self-governing is surely fundamental to ethical counselling practice.

The word 'change' is a very emotive one in the area of same-sex attraction. Personally, I prefer to speak of biblical transformation, which every believer should be experiencing. This transformation may or may not involve a change in the direction of a person's sexual attractions. But becoming hetero-sexual is not the goal of biblical transformation. Rather, it is to be transformed into the likeness of Jesus Christ: 'And we all, who with unveiled faces contemplate the Lord's glory, are being transformed into his image with ever-increasing glory, which comes from the Lord, who is the Spirit' (2 Corinthians 3:18).

No falling back

I'd been a Christian for less than two years when I was invited by some friends to attend a healing service at a large local church. I went in the eager expectation that the blind would see, the deaf would hear and the lame would walk. But it was a much less spectacular affair. Well, not spectacular at all really. However, what the evening lacked in terms of signs and wonders, the pastor tried to make up for with his zeal and unwavering faith that God would act in healing power.

Towards the end of the evening I went forward tentatively. In response to the question: 'What would you like God to do for you?', I whispered that I wanted to be set free from homosexuality. The pastor assured me that if I had enough faith, God would certainly do this. He then prayed over me, as others gathered around and laid hands on me. There was an expectation, for some reason, that I might fall over backwards. I wasn't worried, though, because two sturdy men lay in wait with open arms ready to catch me. But their services weren't required.

Having prayed, the pastor then announced (in a surprisingly loud voice), 'Brother, God has set you free from your homosexuality.' My first reaction was a rather awkward, internal, 'Actually, what I shared was confidential.' I soon forgot my embarrassment though and felt a surge of excitement about my new-found freedom in Christ.

The prayer counsellors urged me to go home and, in effect, to live out my new straight life. Finally!

But my new straight life didn't last long. I remember watching a film starring Tom Cruise and thinking, 'Well, he's just as good-looking as he was before.' Clearly, I was still exclusively same-sex attracted.

So what went wrong? I genuinely believed that God had acted miraculously. But perhaps my faith was insufficient? Or was there some unconfessed sin in my life that prevented God from working? Some well-meaning brothers and sisters put forward each of those explanations at the time.

Living (or dying) by faith

The writer of Hebrews teaches us an important lesson on faith. In chapter 11, sometimes known as the 'gallery of faith', we read of some great things accomplished in and through various Old Testament characters 'by faith'. So Noah, Abraham, Jacob, Joseph and Moses all get a mention, as does the prostitute Rahab. The writer continues,

> And what more shall I say? I do not have time to tell about Gideon, Barak, Samson and Jephthah, about David and Samuel and the prophets, who through faith conquered kingdoms, administered justice, and gained what was promised; who shut the mouths of lions, quenched the fury of the flames, and escaped the edge of the sword; whose weakness was turned to strength; and who became powerful in battle and routed foreign armies. Women received back their dead, raised to life again.
> (Hebrews 11:32–35a)

Isn't this thrilling, riveting stuff? Great acts – many supernatural – all accomplished 'through faith'. My heart is stirred and excited when I read Hebrews 11, as I reflect on the God of the miraculous. The God who, still today, can intervene in people's lives to bring freedom and victory, and who can even raise the dead.

But hold on. The writer hasn't finished yet. There's a sudden gear change down to a much more solemn, sobering note:

There were others who were tortured, refusing to be released so that they might gain an even better resurrection. Some faced jeers and flogging, and even chains and imprisonment. They were put to death by stoning; they were sawn in two; they were killed by the sword. They went about in sheepskins and goatskins, destitute, persecuted and ill-treated – the world was not worthy of them. They wandered in deserts and mountains, living in caves and in holes in the ground.
(verses 35b–38)

Oh. What's gone wrong? This wasn't part of God's plan, was it? Perhaps those who suffered and died and faced persecution had some unconfessed sin in their lives. Or maybe they lacked faith – is that why they're shoved towards the end of the chapter, almost as an embarrassed afterthought?

Absolutely, categorically not! Let's read on:

These were all commended for their faith, yet none of them received what had been promised, since God had planned something better for us so that only together with us would they be made perfect.
(verses 39–40)

Did you notice that little word 'all'? All of the people mentioned in Hebrews 11 were commended for their faith, that is, for trusting God and his promises. So not only the ones who experienced the dramatic interventions and miraculous rescues, but also the ones who were jeered, flogged, tortured, persecuted, imprisoned, stoned to death or sawn in two. They were *all* heroes of faith.

They were all *heroes of faith.*

Satisfaction guaranteed?

God may choose to intervene in your life in some dramatic, unexpected, even miraculous way. He may bring about incredible changes in the life of a same-sex attracted Christian, perhaps enable that person to get married. He may even bring complete freedom from same-sex desires. Our omnipotent (all-powerful) God is able to do that.

But that hasn't been my experience. And it hasn't been Rob's either. Nor is it the testimony of most of the Christians I know who struggle with same-sex temptations. Perhaps it's not your story either. Or that of the friends you are helping. For some, it might be. But whatever God may or may not choose to do in your life, I would urge you to continue walking with Jesus by faith. Make it your passionate goal to pursue ultimate satisfaction in him.

If you continue to deny yourself a same-sex relationship out of love for Jesus Christ, believing that God has planned something better for you in the future, then you too will be commended as a genuine hero of faith. And no matter how difficult the journey, the final destination will bring complete and eternal satisfaction. In this world we get foretastes of the abundant life promised by Jesus, but for the Christian the best is still to come:

> You make known to me the path of life;
>   in your presence there is fullness of joy;
> at your right hand are pleasures for evermore.
> (Psalm 16:11)

APPENDIX I: SUPPORTING PEOPLE FACING SAME-SEX TEMPTATIONS

Some dos

1. **Do** be willing to listen to someone's personal story. Ask lots of questions and show that you're genuinely interested in understanding their struggles and how these impact their faith. But do this sensitively, so that you don't come across as intrusive or as a meddler.
2. **Do** encourage people to draw near to God and involve him in the struggle. God doesn't want to be a distant bystander when we're wrestling with temptations. He wants to be right there with us in the midst of our battles. Encouraging someone to pour out their heart to God is often one of the most helpful things you can do.
3. **Do** be vulnerable and, at an appropriate point, share something of your own personal struggles. Most people don't like to be supported by someone who appears to have life completely sorted! Being real about how you experience God's grace in the midst of personal weaknesses puts both of you on a level footing.

4. **Do** assure people that they're fully loved and accepted in Christ. Many struggling with same-sex temptations will have heard lots of truth from other Christians, but may have experienced very little grace. Help them, through the Scriptures, to grasp the full extent of Christ's love for them.

5. **Do** ask what kind of support and encouragement might be welcome. It's easy to assume that you know what will help someone, but most people really appreciate being asked. Explore what role – if any – you might be able to have in providing encouragement. But be realistic, and don't over-promise!

6. **Do** show grace and mercy if someone admits to you that they have fallen and failed in some way. This will help reassure them that they're loved both by God and by you, even if they slip up. How might God use you in helping to restore them and to encourage them back onto the right path?

7. **Do** encourage the pursuit of practical godliness. Listening, understanding and showing compassion are all vital. But we should also consider how we can spur one another on towards love and good deeds (Hebrews 10:24). All of us need trusted friends who will speak the truth in love and urge us to live godly lives.

8. **Do** open your home and welcome in unmarried people. Single people often really appreciate being made to feel part of someone's family. Could you invite them to special family occasions, for regular meals, on days out, or even to join you on holiday? Such things could be a great blessing.

9. **Do** be prepared to show practical, self-sacrificial love. Ask (tactfully!) if there are any particular needs that you might be able to meet. Someone might appreciate

regular hospitality, or financial help if they're in a one-person household, or they could perhaps benefit from some practical skill that God has entrusted to you.

10. **Do** try to understand their hopes and fears for the future. Knowing what someone is hoping for (e.g. marriage or new friends) will provide helpful insights as you pray. And perhaps you'll be able to offer some constructive, gentle advice. By knowing their fears, you can hopefully encourage them to trust in God and his provision.

Some don'ts

1. **Don't** try to 'fix' people or turn them into a pet project. Most people struggling with same-sex temptations aren't looking to be fixed. They're more likely to appreciate people who fully accept and genuinely care for them. Those who will stand by them in good times and bad, as they try to swim against the cultural tide.

2. **Don't** assume that you know what causes them to experience same-sex attractions. Causation theories are many and varied, and multiple factors might contribute to someone experiencing attractions to the same sex. So, biological/genetic factors, for example, or psychological, environmental and social factors. Don't take one particular causation theory and dogmatically apply it to their personal story.

3. **Don't** elevate same-sex practice and make it appear to be worse than other sins. We are all redeemed sinners and we all continue to battle against various temptations. Same-sex temptations are not in a league of their own, and those struggling with them are not 'special cases' that need to be treated differently.

4. **Don't** be afraid to return to the topic again when someone shares their struggle with same-sex desires. They might be feeling insecure, and fearing rejection after revealing something so personal. Or they might simply appreciate an occasional enquiry as to how things are going, or how you could be praying for them.

5. **Don't** make unbiblical promises, as they can shipwreck people's faith. If the Bible doesn't guarantee something, we have no right to hold out a guarantee either. So don't promise, for example, that God will take away someone's same-sex desires and enable them to get married. Instead, encourage them with truly biblical promises.

6. **Don't** downplay the gift of singleness. For people with same-sex temptations, singleness may not be the gift they would choose. But try sensitively to encourage them to see that they can use the freedom of their unmarried state to devote themselves to God and to gospel work.

7. **Don't** be automatically suspicious of every close same-sex friendship. Christians struggling with same-sex temptations need good and godly friends to help them stick to the narrow road that leads to life. This includes same-sex friends. There are dangers, of course, but don't rush to assume the worst when two people are close.

8. **Don't** be afraid to gently warn people, especially if someone is being deceived and going astray. This has to be done really carefully, of course, out of a heart full of love rather than harsh judgment. And before you even contemplate challenging someone else's behaviour, ensure you remove any planks from your own eye.

9. **Don't** neglect to pray for the person struggling in this area. Pray for them to be full of the Holy Spirit so that they can resist temptation. Pray for them to know God's grace and love in abundance, for their delight in Christ to grow, for God to provide all that they need to sustain them in this battle. Regular prayer can release God's transforming power into their lives.

10. **Don't** forget to remind people that the Christian life involves sacrifice. Jesus never promises that his followers will have an easy life. We're called to deny ourselves, take up our cross and follow him. Are you able to model a life of sacrifice that will serve as an inspiration to someone facing same-sex temptations?

APPENDIX II: RESOURCES AND FURTHER READING

Resources

Living Out livingout.org
Coordinated by three Christian leaders who experience same-sex attraction. Stories, resources and questions to help gay people and Christians who struggle with same-sex temptations.

Satisfied in Christ satisfiedinchrist.com
Jonathan and Rob's blog. Regular articles to provide encouragement for all Christians, single or married, same-sex or opposite-sex attracted. Aiming to inspire us all to make Christ our greatest treasure and to pursue ultimate satisfaction in and through our relationship with him.

True Freedom Trust truefreedomtrust.co.uk
UK-based teaching and pastoral support ministry for Christians struggling with issues around same-sex attraction, and for their families, friends and church leaders. Can provide speakers and lecturers for Bible colleges, churches, conferences, youth groups and so on.

Further reading

Sam Allberry, *Is God Anti-Gay?* (The Good Book Company, 2013)

Rosaria Champagne Butterfield, *The Secret Thoughts of an Unlikely Convert: An English Professor's Journey into Christian Faith* (Crown & Covenant Publications, 2012)

Kevin DeYoung, *What Does the Bible Really Teach about Homosexuality?* (IVP, 2015)

Ed Shaw, *The Plausibility Problem: The Church and Same-Sex Attraction* (IVP, 2015)

Preston Sprinkle, *People to Be Loved: Why Homosexuality Is Not Just an Issue* (Zondervan, 2016)

Mark A. Yarhouse, PsyD, *Homosexuality and the Christian: A Guide for Parents, Pastors and Friends* (Bethany House Publishers, 2010)

NOTES

1. Craving counterfeit gods

1. Charles Wesley, 'And Can It Be That I Should Gain?', *Psalms and Hymns* (1738).

2. Manufacturing idols

1. John Calvin, *Institutes of the Christian Religion*, trans. F. L. Battles (Westminster Press, 1960), I: 11.8.

2. C. S. Lewis, *The Weight of Glory* (HarperCollins, 2013), Kindle edn.

3. Kassia Wosick, Assistant Professor of Sociology at New Mexico State University, http://www.nbcnews.com/business/business-news/porn-industry-feeling-upbeat-about-2014-n9076.

4. John Piper, http://www.desiringgod.org/interviews/what-is-god-s-glory.

5. Athanasius, *On The Incarnation* (Christian Classics Ethereal Library, 2009), Kindle edn, ch 3: 'The Divine Dilemma and Its Solution in the Incarnation – Continued'.

6. William Cowper, 'O for a Closer Walk with God' (1772).

3. A jealous God – and second chances

1. Oliver Stone interview, Conversations with History; Institute of International Studies, University of California, Berkeley: globetrotter.berkeley.edu/conversations/Stone/stone-con6.html.
2. William Shakespeare, *Othello*, III.3.
3. Oprah Winfrey, https://www.youtube.com/watch?v=Oxao4LmTMfU.
4. Westminster Shorter Catechism: Answer to Q. 1, What is the chief end of man?
5. http://www.unionsanitary.com/whatsNew.htm.
6. http://www.thetimes.co.uk/tto/science/article4314070.ece.
7. John Piper, *Desiring God: Meditations of a Christian Hedonist*, rev. edn (Multnomah, 2011), Kindle edn, ch. 10.

4. Did God really say . . . ?

1. http://edition.cnn.com/SHOWBIZ/9704/06/ellen.
2. http://www.theguardian.com/music/2014/may/29/sam-smith-debut-in-the-lonely-hour-album-written-about-guy.
3. http://www.independent.co.uk/news/people/sir-elton-john-says-jesus-would-support-gay-marriage-he-was-all-about-love-9571113.html.
4. A. J. Jacobs, *The Year of Living Biblically* (Random House, 2009), Kindle edn. Examples are taken from September and January.
5. Tom Daley, https://www.youtube.com/watch?v=OJwJnoB9EKw.

5. Everything you need?

1. J. B. Phillips, *Your God Is Too Small: A Guide for Believers and Skeptics Alike* (Touchstone, 2004), p. 63.
2. Itzhak Bars and John Terning, *Extra Dimensions in Space and Time* (Springer, 2009), p. 27.
3. http://journal.frontiersin.org/article/10.3389/neuro.09.031.2009/full.

4. http://discovermagazine.com/2011/apr/20-things-you-didnt-know-about-dna.

5. Horatius Bonar, 'I Heard the Voice of Jesus Say' (1846).

6. John Flavel, 'Christ Is to Be Loved', in *The Essential Works of John Flavel* (GLH Publishing, 2012), Kindle edn.

7. Oscar Wilde, *The Picture of Dorian Gray* (Public Domain, 1994), Kindle edn, ch. 2.

8. C. S. Lewis, *Mere Christianity* (HarperCollins, 2009), Kindle edn, ch. 11, 'Faith'.

9. Charitie L. Bancroft, 'Before the Throne of God Above' (1863).

6. Gripped by grace

1. http://solarsystem.nasa.gov/planets/earth/facts.

2. Charles Wesley, 'O for a Thousand Tongues to Sing' (1739).

3. John Newton, 'Amazing Grace' (1779).

4. D. Martyn Lloyd-Jones, *Spiritual Depression: Its Causes and Cure* (Marshall Pickering, 2015), Kindle edn, ch. 2.

7. Blurred vision

1. Facebook Diversity page, https://www.facebook.com/facebookdiversity/posts/638787136217792?fref=nf (27 June 2014).

2. Foresight Future Identities (2013): Final Project Report. The Government Office for Science, London.

8. Living sacrifice

1. http://sheu.org.uk/content/page/young-people-2014.

9. Useful to the Master

1. See 2 Corinthians 10:10; 11:16–33; 12:1–7.

2. Richard Sibbes, *The Bruised Reed* (1630), Kindle edn, ch. 13, 'Grace Shall Reign'.

3. Charles H. Spurgeon, Sermon 222, 7 November 1858, http://www.romans45.org/spurgeon/sermons/0222.htm.

4. Charles H. Spurgeon, 'The Minister's Fainting Fits', *Lectures to My Students* (Banner of Truth, 2008), Kindle edn, ch. XI.

5. William Still, in David Searle (ed.), *Truth and Love in a Sexually Disordered World* (Paternoster, 1997), p. 51.

10. Pursuing intimacy with God

1. Alain de Botton, https://twitter.com/alaindebotton/status/395667117774610434.

2. Gene Weingarten, 'Pearls before Breakfast', *Washington Post*, 8 April 2007.

11. Enjoying intimacy with others

1. C. S. Lewis, *The Four Loves* (HarperCollins, 2010), Kindle edn, ch. 4, 'Friendship'.

2. http://content.time.com/time/specials/packages/article/0,28804,1939342_1939424_1939709,00.html.

12. The gift of being unmarried

1. Office for National Statistics, Marriages in England and Wales, 2010 (http://www.ons.gov.uk/ons/rel/vsob1/marriages-in-england-and-wales--provisional-/2010/marriages-in-england-and-wales--2010.html).

2. Office for National Statistics, Living Alone in England and Wales, Part of 2011 Census Analysis (http://www.ons.gov.uk/ons/rel/census/2011-census-analysis/do-the-demographic-and-socio-economic-characteristics-of-those-living-alone-in-england-and-wales-differ-from-the-general-population-/sty-living-alone-in-the-uk.html).

13. The future of marriage

1. Timothy Keller, with Kathy Keller, *The Meaning of Marriage: Facing the Complexities of Commitment with the Wisdom of God* (Hodder & Stoughton, 2013), Kindle edn, ch. 3.

2. One of the Prefaces to the Church of England's marriage service.

3. http://truefreedomtrust.co.uk/contact_form.

4. For example, Christopher Ash, *Married for God* (IVP, 2007); Tim Keller, *The Meaning of Marriage* (Hodder & Stoughton, 2013); Paul Tripp, *What Did You Expect?* (IVP, 2010).